Inventing Popular Culture

Blackwell Manifestos

In this new series major critics make timely interventions to address important concepts and subjects, including topics as diverse as, for example: Culture, Race, Religion, History, Society, Geography, Literature, Literary Theory, Shakespeare, Cinema, and Modernism. Written accessibly and with verve and spirit, these books follow no uniform prescription but set out to engage and challenge the broadest range of readers, from undergraduates to postgraduates, university teachers and general readers – all those, in short, interested in ongoing debates and controversies in the humanities and social sciences.

Already Published

The Idea of Culture
Terry Eagleton

The Future of Christianity
Alister E. McGrath

Reading After Theory
Valentine Cunningham

21st-Century Modernism
Marjorie Perloff

The Future of Theory
Jean-Michel Rabaté

Inventing Popular Culture
John Storey

Forthcoming

The Idea of Latin America
Walter Mignolo

The Future of Society
William Outhwaite

The Death of Race
David Goldberg

Biography: The Facts
Hermione Lee

The Idea of Black Culture
Hortense Spillers

The Idea of Shakespeare
Bruce Smith

Inventing Popular Culture

From Folklore to Globalization

John Storey

Blackwell
Publishing

BLACKWELL PUBLISHING
350 Main Street, Malden, MA 02148-5020, USA
9600 Garsington Road, Oxford OX4 2DQ, UK
550 Swanston Street, Carlton, Victoria 3053, Australia

First published 2003 by Blackwell Publishing Ltd

6   2008

Library of Congress Cataloging-in-Publication Data

Storey, John, 1950–
    Inventing popular culture : from folklore to globalization / John Storey.
        p. cm. — (Blackwell manifestos)
Includes bibliographical references and index.
    ISBN 978-0-631-23459-3 (hardcover : alk. paper) – ISBN 978-0-631-23460-9
(pbk : alk. paper)
1. Popular culture. 2. Popular culture—Philosophy. 3. Culture—Philosophy. I.
Title. II. Series.

CB19.S7455 2003
306—dc21

                                                                    2002156371

A catalogue record for this title is available from the British Library.

Set in 11.5 / 13.5 pt Bembo
by Graphicraft Ltd, Hong Kong
Printed and bound in Singapore
by COS Printers Pte Ltd

For further information on
Blackwell Publishing, visit our website:
www.blackwellpublishing.com

For Jenny and Katie

Contents

Preface   ix

Acknowledgments   xiii

1 Popular Culture as Folk Culture   **1**
Nature and Nationalism   2
Pastoral Life as Primitive Culture   6
Music Hall and the Masses   10
Imagining the Past to Make the Present   13

2 Popular Culture as Mass Culture   **16**
Culture Against Anarchy   16
The Culture of Hyperdemocracy   24
The Marxist Masses   27
Ways of Seeing Other People as Masses   30

3 Popular Culture as the "Other" of High Culture   **32**
The Making of High Culture   32
The Modernist Revolution   41
The Politics of Cultural Exclusion   43
Culture and Class   45

4 Popular Culture as an Arena of Hegemony   **48**
Hegemony: From Marxism to Cultural Studies   48
Wandering from the Path of Righteousness   53

Contents

Side Saddle on the Golden Calf   56
An Inclusive Cultural Studies   61

5 Popular Culture as Postmodern Culture   **63**
The New Sensibility   63
Weird Scenes Inside the Goldmine:
   The Postmodern Condition   64
Postmodern Hyperconsciousness   70
Back to the Future: Opera Postmodern?   74

6 Popular Culture as the "Roots" and "Routes"
of Cultural Identities   **78**
Postmodern Identities   79
The Roots of Cultural Identities   81
The Routes of Cultural Identities   86
Mixing Memory and Desire: Dusty Springfield
   and "The Land of Love"   89
Coda: Performing Identities   91

7 Popular Culture as Popular or Mass Art   **92**
Cultural Power   92
When Gravity Fails: An Aesthetics of Popular
   Culture?   95
Beyond Aesthetic Essentialism   104

8 Popular Culture as Global Culture   **107**
Globalization   107
Trading Commodities for Culture in the American
   Global Village   109
The "Local" as the New Folk Culture   116

Notes   121

References   130

Index   140

Preface

Inventing Popular Culture is written from the critical perspective of cultural studies. Cultural studies works with an inclusive definition of culture. That is, it is a "democratic" project in the sense that rather than studying only what Matthew Arnold called "the best which has been thought and said" (1960: 6), cultural studies is committed, in principle, to examining *all* that has been thought and said.

In very broad terms, culture is how we live nature (including our own biology). To say that culture is how we live nature will sound to many people like a hopelessly inclusive way to conceptualize culture. But the world is full of seemingly hopelessly inclusive concepts. Think of the concept of history defined as the study of the past. Hopelessly inclusive? What historians do in practice is recognize the concept at its level of generality, but then limit their investigation to the level of the particular. Similarly, to have a degree in English literature, for example, does not mean that someone has studied all of the ever-changing object of study which counts as English literature. But English literature still continues to exist as an object of study. In the same way, then, to study culture (defined as how we live nature) is not to embark on an examination of all the changing ways we live (and have lived) nature but to focus on particular ways. In this it is no different from most forms of analysis which work from the general to the particular (and then sometimes back to the general).

Culture is an active process. It does not lie dormant in things (that is, any commodity, object, or event that can be made to signify), waiting patiently to be woken by an appropriate consumer. It is the practice of making and communicating meanings. Culture is not in the object but in the experience of the object: how we make it meaningful, what we do with it, how we value it, etc. "Culture is ordinary" (Williams 1958a): it is how we make sense of ourselves and the world around us; it is the practice through which we share and contest meanings of ourselves, of each other, and of the world. Watching a soap opera and talking about what the characters are doing; arguing about who should have won a football match; remembering together the songs of a shared youth; debating the claims of politicians and big business; protesting at the injustices and economic inequalities of globalization. In these, and in many other ways, we make and share meanings. To modify and paraphrase Karl Marx (1977), we make meanings and we are made by meanings. To share a culture is to interpret the world – to make it meaningful – in recognizably similar ways.

To see culture, however, as the practices and processes of making shared meanings does not mean that cultural studies believes that cultures are harmonious, organic wholes. On the contrary, cultures are both shared and conflicting networks of meanings. Cultures are arenas in which different ways of articulating the world come into conflict and alliance. The fact that meaning is not something fixed and guaranteed in nature, but is always the result of particular ways of representing nature in culture, suggests that the meaning of something can never be fixed, final, or true; its meaning will only ever be contextual and contingent and, moreover, always open to the changing relations of power.

Therefore, although the world certainly exists in all its enabling and constraining materiality outside representation, it is only in practices of representation that the world can be made to mean. Representation constructs the reality it appears only to describe. It is never a simple question of what is true or false but of what counts as "truth." Ideologies are discourses which attempt to impose closure on meaning in the interests of power; to make what is cultural (i.e. made) appear as nature. Furthermore, dominant ways of making the world meaningful, produced by those with the power to make their ways of articulating meaning circulate discursively in the world, generate the "hegemonic truths" which seek to assume an authority over the ways in which we think and act; that is, they invite us to take up "subject positions" from which meanings can be made and actions carried out. It is this conflict – the relations between culture and power – which is the core interest of cultural studies.

The version of cultural studies I advocate here is Gramscian (see especially chapter 4 and Storey 1999). From this perspective, the cultural field is marked by a struggle to articulate, disarticulate, and rearticulate particular meanings, particular ideologies, particular politics. Meaning is always a social production, a human practice; and because different meanings can be ascribed to the same thing, meaning is always the site and the result of struggle. The problem with "economic reductionism" (meaning is determined by its mode of production) and "textual essentialism" (meaning is an inherent property of things) is that they drain the world of the activity and the agency which go into the making of meaning, and in so doing they simplify "the politics of culture." However, although the distinction between, say, high and popular culture (a key concern of this book) has no basis in textual properties or modes of production, this should not lead us to ignore the institutional embeddedness of this distinction. What should be examined, therefore, is not the distinction at the level of textuality or mode of production, but how the distinction is maintained and deployed in strategies of power.

Inventing Popular Culture is about the idea of popular culture, the different ways in which popular culture has been defined for analysis. Like French historian Roger Chartier (1993), I will argue that popular culture is a category invented by intellectuals. Popular culture may be found in earlier historical periods, but the concept only emerges in the late eighteenth century in intellectual accounts of "folk" culture. My argument about popular culture is the same as that made by Raymond Williams in relation to social class. As Williams (1993) points out, "It is obvious, of course, that this spectacular history of the new use of *class* does not indicate the *beginning* of social divisions in England. But it indicates, quite clearly, a change in the character of these divisions, and it records, equally clearly, a change in attitudes towards them" (xv). What Williams says about class can also be said about popular culture.

Inventing Popular Culture, therefore, will not present an analysis of particular texts which can be defined as popular culture; instead it will explore the changing intellectual ways of constructing texts as popular culture and how these intellectual discourses articulate questions of culture and power. As we shall see, debates about popular culture are rarely if ever focused only on forms of entertainment: the idea of popular culture is always entangled with questions of social power, especially in terms of claims and counter-claims about, for example, class, gender, ethnicity, "race," generation, and sexuality. Each chapter will examine a different way of thinking about popular culture. In particular, the book will explore the ways in which the idea of popular culture is often a way of categorizing and dismissing the cultural practices of "ordinary" people. Although the term popular culture can be articulated to carry a range of different meanings, what all these have in common is the idea of *popularis* – belonging to the people. Therefore, each of the different ways in which popular culture is formulated always carries with it a definition of "the people."

In *Culture and Society* (first published in 1958), Williams observed, "we live in an expanding culture, yet we spend much of our energy regretting the fact, rather than seeking to understand its nature and conditions" (1993: iv). The most common term for this expanding culture is popular culture. The final aim of *Inventing Popular Culture* is to explore the energy that has been spent on regretting the development of our expanding culture.

Acknowledgments

First of all I would like to thank Jayne Fargnoli for inviting me to write this book. I would also like to thank all my colleagues in the Department of Media and Cultural Studies and the Centre for Research in Media and Cultural Studies, University of Sunderland, for bearing the additional (and often invisible) burdens that some-one taking research leave always leaves behind. Special thanks to Dr Shaun Moores, Dr Tony Purvis, and Dr Angela Werndly, who between them covered my teaching and yet still found time to talk to me about many of the themes of this book. Also special thanks to all the students I have worked with and learned from during my 12 years at the University of Sunderland. Finally, my deepest thanks to Jenny and Katie, without whom, quite simply, "winter would hold no spring."

1

Popular Culture as Folk Culture

In the late eighteenth, throughout the nineteenth, and into the early part of the twentieth century, different groups of intellectuals, working under the different banners of nationalism, Romanticism, folklore, and finally, folk song, "invented" the first concept of popular culture. In fact, these debates eventually produced two definitions of popular culture. The first was popular culture as a quasi-mythical rural "folk culture," and the other – and it was very much the "other" – was popular culture as the degraded "mass culture" of the new urban-industrial working class.[1]

The culture of the "common people" has always been an object of concern for men and women with social and political power. However, in the late eighteenth and early nineteenth centuries, as "traditional" popular culture, and the "traditional" cultural relations between dominant and subordinate classes, began to collapse under the sweeping impact of industrialization, urbanization, and the emergence of an urban-industrial working class, many European and American intellectuals started to take a special interest in the culture of the "folk" (Burke 1996). Middle-class men and women began to demand stories and songs from the people from whom they had previously demanded only labor and respect. In this way, then, folk culture was very much a category of the learned, constructed by intellectuals, especially collectors, editors, and publishers, and not a concept generated by the people defined as the folk.

The collecting of, and the theorizing about, the culture of the folk occurs in two historical periods. The first period (when the objects of collection and study were "ballad" and "folk tales") began with the publication of Thomas Percy's *Reliques of Ancient English Poetry* in 1765 and ended with Francis James Child's *The English and Scottish Popular Ballads* (the first volume of the first edition was published in 1857, the third edition in 1898). The second period (when the object of collection and study was the "folk song") began with the publication of Carl Engel's *An Introduction to the Study of National Music* (1866) and ended with the publication in 1907 of Cecil James Sharp's *Folksong: Some Conclusions*.[2]

Nature and Nationalism

The "discovery" of folk culture was an integral part of emerging European nationalisms. The role of the actual folk – rural workers – was mainly symbolic. As we shall see, they were the mere carriers of something they did not really understand; the embodiment of a way of life that they themselves were increasingly powerless to sustain. From the very influential work of Johann Gottfried Herder in the 1770s to the last major contribution to the debate on folk song, that of Sharp in 1907, we find the same idea repeated over and over again: folk culture is the very embodiment of the nature and character of a nation. For this reason, if for no other, it should be collected and treasured.

In Herder's work on folk culture the natural and the national blur. The value of *Volkslied* (folk or people's song), in its spontaneity and simplicity, is that it is almost an outgrowth of nature: it is the nature in which the culture of the nation can be grown. Herder argued that folk song still possessed what all poetry had once possessed – a moral or civilizing function. Folk song thus represented a fundamental challenge to artificial and inauthentic modes of living. As such it suggested the possibility of a return to a more "grounded" or "rooted" culture; a return to culture before the Fall into the corrupting conditions of industrialization and urbanization, which for Herder was producing artificiality at the "top" and degradation at the "bottom" of society. But because the music of the folk belonged to a time before the Fall, it carried within it the possibility of purification; the soul of the nation could be made to rise above the contamination and corruption of a mechanical and material civilization. He therefore urged intellectuals to follow his example (of 1774 and 1778) and make collections of the poetry of the folk.

Like Herder, the folk-tale collectors Jacob and Wilhelm Grimm believed that folk culture provided access to the origins of, and the possibility of a return to, an authentic German cultural identity. Although industrialization and urbanization threatened to sweep away what little remained of folk culture, there was still time to collect and preserve this vital and valuable heritage before it disappeared forever. In the preface to the first edition of *Household and Children's Tales* (1812), the Grimms presented their collection in the language of a romantic allegory:

> when the heavens have unleashed a storm, or when some other natural disaster has battered down a whole harvest, we may well find that in some sheltered corner by the roadside, under hedges and shrubs, a few ears of corn have survived. When the sun begins to shine again, they will grow, hidden and unnoticed. No early scythe will cut them for the cornhouses. Only late in summer when the ears are ripe and heavy with grain, some poor humble hand will glean them, and bind them carefully, one by one. The little bundles will be carried home, more cherished than big sheaves, and will provide food for the winter, and perhaps the only seed for the future. (quoted in Michaelis-Jena 1970: 52–3)

The harvest that had been battered down by urbanization and industrialization had left behind the remains of a simpler time of

3

"kings, princes, faithful servants and honest craftsmen" (53). With these remains it may be possible to provide food for the winter and seed for a better future. They were not alone in this hope. As one Finnish intellectual proclaimed in 1809, "No fatherland can exist without folk poetry. [It] . . . is nothing more than the crystal in which a nationality can mirror itself; it is the spring which brings to the surface the truly original in the folk soul" (quoted in Burke 1996: 12).

Peter Burke (1996) argues that between 1500 and 1800 there occurred a remarkable change in the attitude of members of the dominant class toward the culture of subordinate classes. As he explains,

> In 1500, they despised the common people, but shared their culture. By 1800 their descendants had ceased to participate spontaneously in popular culture, but they were in the process of rediscovering it as something exotic and therefore interesting. They were even beginning to admire "the people", from whom this alien culture had sprung. (286)

Although in general terms this is undoubtedly true, we need to remember that "the people" they admired were a people safely in the past; "the people" of the urban present were still despised.[3] Therefore, although Herder and the other collectors appear to argue against the more traditional view of "lower-class" culture as little more than the fallen sweepings of what had once belonged to the dominant classes, this did not mean that they saw all "ordinary people" – those who still sang the songs and told the tales – as the very embodiment of both the nature and the character of the nation. In his collection *Folk Songs* (1778), Herder was at pains to make a clear distinction, one which became the model for all future collections and comments on collections, between the urban "rabble" and the rural "people." As he explained, " 'People' does not mean the rabble in the streets, which never sings or creates but rather screams and mutilates true folk songs" (quoted in Clark 1969:

259). A similar point is made by William Motherwell (*Minstrelsy: Ancient and Modern*, 1827). He claims that traditional songs (what others – mostly later – would call folk songs) were the progeny of "the patriotick children of an ancient and heroick race," who should not be confused with the urban "rabble." Motherwell, like the brothers Grimm, feared that "opportunities of recovering traditional song" were disappearing because of the way "changes . . . within this half century [have affected] the manners and habits of our peasantry and labouring classes, with whom this song has been cherished." The problem was that working people had "departed from the stern simplicity of their fathers, and have learned with the paltry philosophers, political quacks, and illuminated dreamers on Economick and Moral science, to laugh at the prejudices, beliefs, and superstitions of elder times" (quoted in Harker 1985: 56). Pushing this argument a little further, Francis James Child (1857) denies the folk any role in the production of folk songs (which he calls "popular ballads"): "the popular ballad is not originally the product or the property of the lower orders of the people" (quoted in Hart 1906: 757). Such a fact is "obvious"; the ballad has its origins with the "class whose acts and fortunes they depict – the upper class – though the growth of civilisation has driven them from the memory of the highly polished and instructed, and has left them as an exclusive possession to the uneducated."

Whether or not folk culture had been produced by the peasantry, it was an inheritance which they had already begun to neglect. Increasingly, the peasantry, like the urban rabble, could not be trusted with the nation's folk heritage. Fortunately, the middle-class collector was at hand. It was imperative that middle-class intellectuals assumed control of folk culture on behalf of the nation. This was joyously welcomed by the honest and deferential peasant of the middle-class imaginary. Sharp (1907) invites us to

> *Imagine*, then, the joy when the collector calls upon them [the honest and deferential peasants] and tells them of his love of the old ditties. He has only to convince them of his sincerity

5

to have them at his mercy. They will sing to him in their old quavering voices until they can sing no more; and, when he is gone, they will ransack their memories that they may give him of their best, should, perchance, he call again, as he promised. (106; my italics)

Pastoral Life as Primitive Culture

Whether or not folk culture was understood as a product of the folk or merely something they had preserved, unaware of its true value, one thing that all the intellectuals involved agreed on, collectors and those who commented on the collections, was that production or preservation had only been possible because the folk had survived in primitive rural isolation. This fact alone made the rapid spread of industrialization and urbanization such a worrying development.

In *Primitive Culture* (1871), Sir Edward Burnet Tylor argued that folklore was a "survival" of an earlier savage culture shared by all social classes. Although European societies, according to Tylor, are now marked by a division between "the irrational beliefs and practices of the . . . peasantry" and "the enlightened views of the educated classes," folklore "preserved the fragments of an ancient, lower culture, the culture of primitive man" (quoted in Dorson 1968: 193). Although most of humankind was everywhere destined to travel from savagery through barbarism to civilization, there would always be those groups for whom the journey appears to stop at a particular stage. As a result, "we may draw a picture where there shall be scarce a hand's breadth of difference between an English ploughman and a negro of Central Africa" (194). In other words, civilization had marched on, leaving behind, in the beliefs and practices of "peasants" and "savages," the fragmented remains of a once shared antiquity – a reminder to the "educated" (i.e. the dominant classes) of what they had once been and what still remained in both the colonies and the threatening darkness of the new industrial towns and cities of Europe and the USA.

6

The influence of Tylor's idea of cultural survivals on the development of the study of folklore was profound. He was a founding member of the Folk-Lore Society, serving on its council and as Vice-President. As Richard Dorson (1968: 196) observes, in the early work of the members of the Folk-Lore Society "the name of Tylor echoes like that of a household god." Under Tylor's influence, the Folk-Lore Society aimed "to establish a science devoted to reconstructing the world view of pre-historic savages from the contemporary lore of peasants" (202). As another leading member of the society, Andrew Lang, explained, "the method of folklore is . . . to compare" practices and beliefs found in "civilized" countries with those found in "uncivilized countries." Furthermore, "when an apparently irrational and anomalous custom is found in any country, to look for a country where . . . the practice is . . . in harmony with the manners and ideas of the people among whom it prevails" (quoted in Dorson 1968: 206).

The "savage" provided the means to understand the "peasant." As Dorson (1968: 212) observes: "In late Victorian England, a perfect situation existed within the framework of Empire to pursue this end." In the first annual report of the Folk-Lore Society (1879), George Laurence Gomme declared:

> The Folk-Lore survivals of civilisation and the Folk-Status of savage tribes both, therefore, belong to the primitive history of mankind; and in collecting and printing these relics of one epoch, from two widely different sources, the Folk-Lore Society will produce that necessary comparison and illustration which is of so much service to the anthropologist. (quoted in Dorson 1968: 223)

Little wonder, then, that when Edward Clodd was elected President of the Folk-Lore Society in 1895, he was able to observe with confidence, "we have but to scratch the rustic to find the barbarian underneath" (250). The widespread dispersion of such a discourse allowed Ralph Vaughan Williams to claim in 1912, without any hint of irony, "I am a psychical researcher who has actually seen a ghost, for I have been among the more primitive people of England and have noted down their songs" (quoted in Gammon 1980: 83). Similarly, when Samuel Johnson and James Boswell toured the Western Islands of Scotland in 1773, in search of what remained of "pastoral life" and "primitive customs," they concluded that the people they had encountered "were as black and wild in their appearance as any American savages" (quoted in Burke 1996: 8). However, when they visited the Hebrides, their host in one village where they stayed was bitterly offended by their expectation of primitivism: "his pride seemed to be much piqued that we were surprised at his having books" (quoted in Burke 1992: 303).

The later we look in the nineteenth century, the more difficult it becomes to sustain the idea of an isolated folk living in conditions of primitive pastoralism beyond the reach of the modern world. If we think of the enormous changes in transport, communication, and modes of popular entertainment which took place in the nineteenth century, not to mention the travelling performers who had made a living entertaining country people from at least the Middle Ages, it is especially difficult to take seriously the claims made by Sharp in 1907. According to him,

> The expression "common people" is used . . . strictly in its scientific sense [*sic*], to connote those whose mental development has been due not to any formal system of training or education, but solely to environment, communal association, and direct contact with the ups and downs of life . . . [T]he "common people" are the unlettered, whose faculties have undergone no formal training whatsoever, and who have never been brought into close enough contact with educated persons to be influenced by them. (3–4)

It might be possible to sustain such an argument if the people he called the common people had always existed in isolated rural enclaves. However, this is not Sharp's argument. Somewhat unconvincingly he elaborates: "In bygone days, the 'common people' formed no inconsiderable part of the population, and were fairly evenly distributed between urban and country districts" (4). It is very difficult to maintain a position which insists that people living in urban districts "have undergone no formal training whatsoever, and . . . have never been brought into close enough contact with educated persons to be influenced by them." This is little short of willful fantasy.

Romanticism also dreamed of a return to the simple virtues of nature as a means to combat and overcome the artificiality and savagery of urban and industrial life. This is very clear in one of the key documents of English Romanticism, William Wordsworth's *Preface to Lyrical Ballads* (1802). Wordsworth argues that poetry should be written in "the real language of men" as opposed to "the gaudiness and inane phraseology of many modern writers" (1973: 594, 595). He summarizes his position like this,

> The principal object, then, which I proposed to myself in these poems was to choose incidents and situations from common life and to relate or describe them . . . in a selection of language really used by men . . . Low and rustic life was generally chosen, because in that condition, the essential passions of the heart find a better soil in which they can attain their maturity, are less under restraint, and speak a plainer and more emphatic language; because in that condition of life our elementary feelings co-exist in a state of greater simplicity . . . because such men hourly communicate with the best objects from which the best part of language is originally derived. (598)

Wordsworth's return to nature is in effect a call to embed culture back in the soil from which the concept had first developed. The call to return to nature was also a critique and rejection of urbanization and industrialization and the culture to which it had supposedly given birth. As he explains, in a passage which echoes through the later work of many of the critics of so-called "mass culture" (see chapter 2),

> a multitude of causes, unknown to former times, are now acting with a combined force to blunt the discriminating powers of the mind, and unfitting it for all voluntary exertion to reduce it to a state of almost savage torpor. The most effective of these causes . . . [is] the increasing accumulation of men in cities, where the uniformity of their occupations produces a craving for extraordinary incident, which the rapid communication of intelligence [popular newspapers] hourly gratifies. To this tendency of life and manners the literature [popular fiction] and theatrical exhibitions [stage melodrama and circus] of the country have conformed themselves . . . When I think upon this degrading thirst after outrageous stimulation, I am almost ashamed to have spoken of the feeble effort with which I have endeavoured to counteract it.

Although he worried that poetry might not be enough, he was convinced that a culture reconnected to its origins in nature could work to refresh and renew "the discriminating powers of the mind," which in turn might prove a force to challenge urban and industrial culture and those for whom urban and industrial culture was culture.

Music Hall and the Masses

The collectors of folk culture idealized the past in order to condemn the present. The rural worker – the peasant – was mythologized as a figure of nature, a "noble savage" walking the country lanes and working without complaint the fields of his or her betters – the living evidence of, and a link to, a purer and more stable past. The urban-industrial worker, however, was fixed firmly in the present, completely detached from any salvation the past may have been able to offer. Proof of a fall from grace was there for all to see in the urban-industrial worker's unquenchable taste for the corrupt and corrupting songs of the music hall.

Whereas the middle class could be encouraged to connect to a more organic past by embracing folk songs, the working class would have to be forcefully schooled in folk song in the hope of softening their urban and industrial barbarism, especially as it was made manifest in their enjoyment of the songs of music hall.[4] In his "Inaugural Address to the Folk Song Society" in 1899, Sir Hubert Parry warned his audience that "there is an enemy at the door of folk music which is driving it out, namely, the common popular [music hall] songs of the day; and this enemy is one of the most repulsive and most insidious" (1899: 1). Music hall is presented as symptomatic of the supposedly degraded culture of the urban working class. As he explains,

> If one thinks of the . . . terribly overgrown towns . . . where one sees all around the tawdriness of sham jewellery and shoddy clothes . . . [and] people who, for the most part, have the most false ideals, or none at all . . . who think that the commonest rowdyism is the highest expression of human emotion; it is for them that the modern popular music is made, and it is made with commercial intention out of snippets of musical slang. (1–2)

The problem, however, was not just that music hall was so bad but that it

> will drive out folk-music if we do not save it. For even in country districts where folk-songs linger, the people think themselves behindhand if they do not know the songs of the seething towns; and as soon as the little urchins of distant villages catch the sound of a music hall tune, away goes the hope of their troubling their heads with the old fashioned folk-songs. (2)

11

Unlike the music hall produced by "town civilisation," English folk music is "among the purest products of the human mind." The founding of the Folk Song Society, therefore, "is a hopeful sign": it will

> put on record what loveable qualities there are in unsophistic-ated humanity; and to comfort ourselves by the hope that at bottom, our puzzling friend, Democracy, has permanent qualit-ies hidden away somewhere, which may yet bring it out of the slough which the scramble after false ideals, the strife between the heads that organise and the workmen who execute, and the sordid vulgarity of our great city-population, seem in our pessimistic moments to indicate as its inevitable destiny.

Cecil Sharp (1907: 137) makes a similar argument:

> Flood the streets . . . with folk-tunes, and those, who now vul-garise themselves and others by singing coarse music-hall songs, will soon drop them in favour of the equally attractive but far better tunes of the folk. This will make the streets a pleasanter place for those who have sensitive ears, and will do incalcul-able good in civilising the masses.

In particular, Sharp advocated the introduction of folk songs into elementary schools as a means to civilize the masses. He was in no doubt of their "value as an educational force" (134):

> For, good music purifies, just as bad music vulgarises; indeed, the effect of music upon the minds of children is so subtle and so far-reaching that it is impossible to exaggerate the harmful influence upon character which the singing of coarse and vul-gar tunes may have. Up till now, the street song has had an open field; the music taught in the schools has been hopelessly beaten in the fight for supremacy. But the mind that has fed upon the pure melody of the folk will instinctively detect the

poverty-stricken tunes of the music-hall, and refuse to be capt-
ivated and deluded by their superficial attractiveness. (135)

He also believed, bringing us back to questions of nationalism, that
the "study of folk-song will . . . stimulate the growth of the feeling
of patriotism" (135). Not only are folk songs an educational force,
their presence in the education system would change the practice of
education for the better. As he explains, in an argument that would
have such terrible consequences in Germany in the 1930s,

> Our system of education is, at present, too cosmopolitan; it is
> calculated to produce citizens of the world rather than Eng-
> lishmen. And it is Englishmen, English citizens, that we want.
> How can it be remedied? By taking care, I would suggest, that
> every child born of English parents is, in its earliest years,
> placed in possession of all those things which are the distinct-
> ive products of its race . . . the folk-songs, those simple ditties
> which have sprung like wild flowers from the very hearts of
> our countrymen . . . If every child is placed in possession of . . .
> these race-products, he will know and understand his country
> and his countrymen far better than he does at present; and
> knowing and understanding them he will love them the more,
> realise that he is united to them by the subtle bond of blood
> and of kinship, and become, in the highest sense of the word,
> a better citizen, and a truer patriot. (135–6)

Imagining the Past to Make the Present

In many ways the idea of folk culture was a romantic fantasy,
constructed through denial and distortion. It was a fantasy intended
to heal the wounds of the present and safeguard the future by
promoting a memory of a past which had little existence outside
the intellectual debates of the the late eighteenth, nineteenth, and
early twentieth centuries. Here was a lost world of the authentic, a

13

culture before the fall into industrialization, urbanization, and the unavoidable visibility of class relations. Although folk culture survived in the oral traditions of the folk, they did not really understand the treasure they held, and furthermore, they were disappearing as a group; therefore, it was the task of intellectuals – the true inheritors of folk culture – to secure its continuation, with a view to using it to solve the social and cultural problems produced by industrial capitalism.

The songs of the folk allowed middle-class intellectuals to imagine a lost national and natural identity and to dream of the possibility of a new "authentic" national unity of a people bound together once again by the organic "ties of land and language" (Martin-Barbero 1993: 12). At the center of this fantasy stood an image of "the people" that resembled neither rural folk nor urban masses. What resulted, as this empty, impossible category was valorized, was an active denial of the actual lived cultures of working people, both rural and urban – what the Colombian theorist Jesus Martin-Barbero has described as "abstract inclusion and concrete exclusion" (7).

The concept of popular culture as folk culture was an invention made from ways of seeing the culture of the men and women (and their families) who worked the land as agricultural laborers. It was their stories the collectors called "folk-tales," their dances they called "folk-dances," their songs they called "folk-songs," their traditions they called "folk-lore," a version of their culture they called "folk-culture." These were not terms the rural people used themselves, certainly not before they were told that these were the terms to be used.[5] The pastoral fantasy of the folk offered an alternative to the rather troublesome specter of the urban-industrial working class. In this sense, then, the intellectual cult of the rural folk was a nostalgic fantasy of a time when working people recognized their inferiority and acknowledged due deference to their social superiors. As John Carey (1992: 105) observes of intellectuals of the late nineteenth century, they "preferred peasants to almost any other variety of human being, since they were ecologically sound, and their traditional qualities of dour endurance, respect for their betters and

14

illiteracy meant that the intellectual's superiority was in little danger from them."

The first concept of popular culture was invented with the "discovery" of the folk in the late eighteenth century and in the folklore and folk-song movements of the nineteenth and early twentieth centuries. Over a period of about 140 years the idea of popular culture as folk culture was developed by intellectuals across Europe and the USA. They had not set out to produce a way of thinking about popular culture, but in doing what they did – whether this was seeking to promote national cultures or to develop a science of "primitive man" – the first concept of popular culture was invented. But the study of folklore produced not only a concept of popular culture as folk culture, it also helped to establish the tradition of seeing ordinary people as masses, consuming mass culture. This is the concern of the next chapter.

2

Popular Culture as Mass Culture

Like the discovery of folk culture, the invention of popular culture as mass culture was in part a response to middle-class fears engendered by industrialization, urbanization, and the development of an urban-industrial working class. The new industrial towns and cities of the nineteenth century very quickly evolved clear lines of class segregation, in which residential separation was compounded by the new work relations of industrial capitalism. Such developments, it was argued, could only mean a weakening of social authority and the commercial dismantling of cultural cohesion. It was in this context, and its continuing aftermath, that the study of the culture of "the masses" first emerged.

Culture Against Anarchy

Undoubtedly, both in Europe and the United States, the first really influential presentation of popular culture as mass culture was Matthew Arnold's *Culture and Anarchy* (1869). It was this book which established the tradition of seeing popular culture as mass culture, powerfully putting in place an agenda which remained dominant in cultural debate from the 1860s until at least the 1950s. In Arnold's famous phrase, culture is "the best that has been thought and said in the world," singular and universal, radiating timeless and absolute value (1960: 7). Although it can be attained only by "the disinterested and active use of reading, reflection, and observation, in the endeavour to know the best that can be known" (179), it seems that the attainment of culture is forever out of reach for most people. Arnold can be quite explicit about the social limits of culture and cultivation. For example, in "The Bishop and the Philosopher" (1863):

> The mass of mankind will never have any ardent zeal for seeing things as they are; very inadequate ideas will always satisfy them. On these inadequate ideas reposes, and must repose, the general practice of the world. That is as much as saying that whoever sets himself to see things as they are will find himself one of a very small circle; but it is only by this small circle resolutely doing its own work that adequate ideas will ever get current at all. (1954: 364–5)

He makes much the same point in "The Function of Criticism at the Present Time" (1865):

> The highly instructed few, and not the scantily instructed many, will ever be the organ to the human race of knowledge and truth. Knowledge and truth in the full sense of the words, are not attainable by the great mass of the human race at all. (1977: 43–4)

It would appear that to appreciate culture, one has to be already cultured – making culture look suspiciously like a class privilege. There are three possibilities: one can be born cultured; one can be born with the capacity to become cultured; and one can be born into the majority for whom culture will remain a distant and alien prospect. Arnold's vision is based on a curious paradox: for whom are the cultivated preserving culture, if the majority is unsound and has always been, and will always be, unsound? The inescapable answer seems to be: for themselves, a self-perpetuating cultural elite.

17

All that is required from the rest of us is to recognize our cultural difference and acknowledge cultural deference. The mass of human-kind are forever destined to wallow in "their beer, their gin, and their fun" (1954: 591).

Arnold's idea of culture as "the best which has been thought and said," however, is not quite the obviously universal and self-evident category it might seem at first. In *Culture and Anarchy* (1869), for example, he describes the French linguist Ernest Renan as the "friend of reason and the simple natural truth of things" (1960: 17). Therefore, would the best include Renan's claim that "Nature has made . . . a race of tillers of the soil, the Negro race; treat him with kindness and humanity, and all will be as it should" (quoted in Young 1995: 69)? Would it include Count Gobineau's *Essay on the Inequality of Races* (1855)? Arnold said of Gobineau, "His accom-plishments and intelligence deserve all respect" (quoted in Young 1995: 85). Gobineau claimed that "Civilisation is incommunicable . . . to savages" (107). Perhaps Arnold had Gobineau in mind when he stated that "Science has now made visible to everybody the great and pregnant elements of difference which lie in race" (1960: 141). According to Robert Young (1995: 114), Gobineau argued that Paris and London were marked by "racial anarchy," especially apparent in the working class of these cities. "[C]ivilization," Gobineau argued, "had not really 'penetrated' the lower classes and is incommunicable to them, just as . . . it is to lower races." Moreover,

> "the 'inequality' of races . . . means that the capacity does not exist for every human race to become equal with every other" . . . In Gobineau's account of culture versus anarchy, therefore, there is no possibility of education of any kind effecting a civilising force as there would be for Arnold, precisely because of the permanent differences of intellectual capacity.[1]

I would argue that Arnold's position is a great deal closer to Gobineau's than Young seems to suggest. Arnold divides society into Barbarians (aristocracy), Philistines (middle class), and Populace (working class). He then claims that under "our class divisions, there is a common basis of human nature" (1960: 105). When we examine what Arnold means by a common basis, it becomes clear that his position is almost identical with that of Gobineau. If we imagine the human race existing on an evolutionary continuum with itself at one end and a common ancestor shared with the ape at the other, what Arnold is suggesting is that the aristocracy and middle class are further along the evolutionary continuum than the working class. But more to the point, and this is where the continuum ceases to be a continuum, where the working class is is where they are destined to remain. This is shown quite clearly in his example of the common basis of our human nature. He claims that

> every time that *we* snatch up a vehement opinion in ignorance and passion, every time that *we* long to crush an adversary by sheer violence, every time that *we* are envious, every time that *we* are brutal, every time that *we* adore mere power or success, every time that *we* add *our* voice to swell a blind clamour against some unpopular personage, every time that *we* trample savagely on the fallen [we have] found in *our* own bosom *the eternal spirit* of the Populace. (107; my italics)

According to Arnold, it takes only a little help from "circumstances" to make this "eternal spirit" triumph in both Barbarian and Philistine. Although culture can carefully guide the aristocracy and the middle class away from such "circumstances," for the working class, the class in which "the eternal spirit" is said to reside, culture can bring to them only "a much wanted principle . . . of authority, to counteract the tendency to anarchy which seems to be threatening us" (82). Therefore, although Arnold claims that education is "the road to culture" (209), he does not envisage working-class, middle-class, and aristocratic students all walking down the same road. For the aristocracy, education is to accustom it to decline, to banish it to history as a class. For the middle class, education's essential function is to prepare middle-class children for the power that is to be theirs.

Its aim is to convert "a middle class, narrow, ungenial, and unattractive [into] a cultured, liberalised, ennobled, transformed middle class, [one to whom the working class] may with joy direct its aspirations" (1954: 343). For the working class, education is to civilize it for subordination, deference, and exploitation. Arnold saw working-class schools (primary and elementary) as little more than outposts of civilization in a dark continent of working-class barbarism: "they civilise the neighbourhood where they are placed" (1973: 39). In a letter to his mother, written in 1862, he writes, "the State has an interest in the primary school as a civilising agent, even prior to its interest in it as an instructing agent" (1896: 187). According to Arnold, working-class children had to be civilized before they could be instructed.

For Arnold, popular culture as mass culture is the "anarchy" embodied in the disruptive nature of working-class lived culture. The social function of culture is to police this disruptive presence: the "raw and uncultivated . . . masses" (1960: 76); "the raw and unkindled masses" (69); "our masses . . . quite as raw and uncultivated as the French" (76); "those vast, miserable unmanageable masses of sunken people" (193). The problem is working-class lived culture:

> the working class . . . raw and half developed . . . long lain half hidden amidst its poverty and squalor . . . now issuing from its hiding place to assert an Englishman's heaven born privilege of doing as he likes, and beginning to perplex *us* by marching where it likes, meeting where it likes, bawling what it likes, breaking what it likes. (105; my italics)

A working class which has lost "the strong feudal habits of subordination and deference" (76) is a very dangerous working class. It is, as we have seen, the function of education to restore a sense of subordination and deference. Although education would never bring "culture" to the working class, it might bring discipline, which in turn might remove the temptations of trade unionism, political agitation, and cheap entertainment.

In the 1930s the work of Arnold was rearticulated by a group of English literary intellectuals known today as the Leavisites. They applied Arnold's cultural politics to the supposed "cultural crisis" of the 1930s. As F. R. Leavis (writing in 1933) explains, "For Matthew Arnold it was in some ways less difficult. I am thinking of the so much more desperate plight of culture today" (1998: 13). According to the Leavisites, the twentieth century is marked by an increasing cultural decline, characterized by "standardisation and levelling down" (Leavis and Thompson 1977: 3). It was against this process and its results that "the citizen . . . must be trained to discriminate and to resist" (5).

Like Arnold, the Leavisites believed that "culture has always been in minority keeping" (3). As Leavis and Thompson explain,

> Upon the minority depends our power of profiting by the finest human experience of the past; they keep alive the subtlest and most perishable parts of tradition. Upon them depend the implicit standards that order the finer living of an age, the sense that this is worth more than that, this rather than that is the direction in which to go, that the centre is here rather than there. (5)

What had changed was the status of the cultured minority. No longer could it command cultural deference, no longer was its cultural authority unchallenged. Q. D. Leavis refers to a situation in which "the minority, who had hitherto set the standard of taste without any serious challenge" have experienced a "collapse of authority" (1978: 185, 187). She longs for a time when the masses exhibited an "unquestioning assent to authority" (191). She quotes Edmund Gosse to confirm the seriousness of the situation:

> One danger which I have long foreseen from the spread of the democratic sentiment, is that of the traditions of literary taste, the canons of literature, being reversed with success by a popular vote. Up to the present time, in all parts of the world, the

masses of uneducated or semieducated persons, who form the vast majority of readers, though they cannot and do not appreciate the classics of their race, have been content to acknowledge their traditional supremacy. Of late there have seemed to me to be certain signs, especially in America, of a revolt of the mob against our literary masters . . . If literature is to be judged by a plebiscite and if the plebs recognises its power, it will certainly by degrees cease to support reputations which give it no pleasure and which it cannot comprehend. The revolution against taste, once begun, will land us in irreparable chaos. (quoted in Q. D. Leavis 1978: 190)

According to Leavis and Thompson (writing in 1933), what Gosse had only feared had now come to pass:

I have said earlier that culture has always been in minority keeping. But the minority now is made conscious, not merely of an uncongenial, but of a hostile environment . . . "Civilisation" and "culture" are coming to be antithetical terms. It is not merely that the power and the sense of authority are now divorced from culture, but that some of the most disinterested solicitude for civilisation is apt to be, consciously or unconsciously, inimical to culture. (1977: 26)

The corrupt and corrupting culture of the masses threatened "to land us in irreparable chaos." It was against this threat that Leavisism wrote its manifestos, and planned "to introduce into schools a training in resistance [to mass culture]" (F. R. Leavis 1933: 188–9); and outside schools, to promote a "conscious and directed effort . . . [to] take the form of resistance by an armed and active minority" (Q. D. Leavis 1978: 270). The threat of democracy in matters both cultural and political was a terrifying thought for Leavisism. According to Q. D. Leavis, "The people with power no longer represent intellectual authority and culture" (191). Like Arnold, she sees the collapse of traditional authority coming at the same time as the rise of democracy.

Together they squeeze out the cultured minority and produce a terrain which increasingly becomes more and more favorable to "anarchy."

In a temporary escape from the "irreparable chaos" of the present, Leavisism looked back longingly to a cultural golden age, a mythic rural past, when there was a shared culture uncorrupted by commercial interests – the time of the "organic community" (Leavis and Thompson 1977: 2). Although there was some confusion within Leavisism about when exactly this golden age had actually existed, the Elizabethan period of Shakespeare's theater is the most often cited candidate. F. R. Leavis, for example, writes of Shakespeare belonging "to a genuinely national culture, to a community in which it was possible for the theatre to appeal to the cultivated and the populace at the same time" (1933: 216). How Shakespeare's theater supposedly appealed to both the cultivated and the populace is spelled out by Q. D. Leavis: "the masses were receiving their amusement from above . . . They had to take the same amusements as their betters . . . Happily, they had no choice" (1978: 85). She claims that "the spectator of Elizabethan drama, though he might not be able to follow the 'thought' minutely in the great tragedies, was getting his amusement from the mind and sensibility . . . [of] an artist and not from one of his own class." As a consequence, "There was then no such complete separation as we have . . . between the life of the cultivated and the life of the generality" (264).

Clearly, then, the golden age was not just marked by cultural coherence, but, happily for the Leavisites, a cultural coherence based on authoritarian and hierarchical principles. It was a common culture which gave intellectual stimulation at one end and affective pleasure at the other. This was a mythic world in which everyone knew their place, everyone knew their station in life. In fact, it is the world before the working class lost "the strong feudal habits of subordination and deference" (Arnold 1960: 76). In other words, it is also the mythical world of folk culture.

What we have lost is the organic community with the living culture it embodied. Folk songs, folk dances, Cotswold cottages and handicraft products are signs and expressions of something more: an art of life, a way of living, ordered and patterned, involving social arts, codes of intercourse and a responsive adjustment, growing out of immemorial experience, to the natural environment and the rhythm of the year. (Leavis and Thompson 1977: 1–2)[2]

Although the organic community was gone, the Leavisites believed that its values and standards could be re-created by reading works of great literature. Therefore, in a move reminiscent of Sharp's campaign for the teaching of folk songs (see chapter 1), they made plans to dispatch literary missionaries to establish outposts of culture in universities and schools; their mission was to arm students to resist and wage war against the barbarism of popular culture as mass culture. In short, their mission was to produce an "educated public," which would continue the Arnoldian tradition of keeping in circulation "the best which has been thought and said" (now more or less reduced to the reading of works of great literature).

The Culture of Hyperdemocracy

Although Leavisism represents an enormously influential account of popular culture as mass culture, perhaps the classic statement of the coming of mass culture is to be found in the unintentionally comic paranoia of the Spanish philosopher José Ortega y Gasset. In *The Revolt of the Masses* (1930), Ortega claims that the public life of Europe is dominated by one fact: "This fact is the accession of the masses to complete social power" (1961: 9). He continues, "As the masses, by definition, neither should or can direct their own personal existence, and still less rule society in general, this fact means that actually Europe is suffering from the greatest crisis than can afflict peoples, nations, and civilisation" (9). Part of the problem was that there were just too many people in the places Ortega might wish to go. Towns and cities, hotels and cafés, parks and beaches, theaters and concert halls were all full of people. The more he looked, the more he was overwhelmed with paranoia and disgust: "We see the multitude . . . in possession of the places and the instruments created by civilisation . . . Now, suddenly, they appear . . . in the best places, the relatively refined creations of human culture, previously reserved . . . to minorities" (9–10). The masses had not just lost their feudal habits of deference and subordination, they were everywhere taking control of public life: "the mass has decided to advance to the foreground of social life, to occupy the places, to use the instruments and to enjoy the pleasures hitherto reserved to the few" (13).

The rebellion of the masses had produced what Ortega y Gasset called "hyperdemocracy." The hyperdemocratic rule of the masses, he claims, will paint the world a single shade of gray: "The mass crushes beneath it everything that is different, everything that is excellent, individual, qualified and select" (14). But the masses are not entirely to blame. Like Arnold, who despaired at a middle class "drugged on business" (1977: 83), and the Leavisites, who pointed to the cultural and political failings of the middle class, Ortega refers to the crisis of the masses as in part a consequence of "the desertion of the directing minorities, which is always found on the reverse side of the rebellion of the masses" (1961: 35).

In another move, reminiscent of both Arnold and the Leavisites, he claims that "it has been impossible to do more than instruct the masses in the technique of modern life; it has been impossible to educate them" (39). As a result, the masses are without "genuine ideas, nor is their possession culture" (54). Without culture and education, the masses falsely feel no limit on their existence and no sense of inferiority to their obvious superiors (46, 47). Like Arnold, Ortega fears that the "man" in the mass "has entered upon life to do 'what he jolly well likes'" (78). Again, in a manner similar to Arnold, Ortega presents an "evolutionary theory" of the masses. He claims that the "man" in the mass is "a primitive who has slipped through the wings on to the age-old stage of civilisation" (62). As someone convinced of the existence of "inferior races" (77), Ortega elaborates his argument by pointing to the fact "that in Central Africa the negroes also ride in motor-cars and dose themselves with aspirin" (66). Like the Africans of Ortega y Gasset's imperial imagination, the masses of Europe are "vertical invader[s]." As he explains, "The European who is beginning to predominate . . . must then be, in relation to the complex civilisation into which he has been born, a primitive man, a barbarian appearing on the stage through the trap-door, [a] 'vertical invader'" (66).

Although T. S. Eliot (writing in 1948) shared many of the conservative cultural concerns of Arnold and the Leavisites, he rejected the fantasy of "missionary" work: "For there is no doubt that in our headlong rush to educate everyone, we are lowering our standards . . . [and doing this, we] make ready the ground upon which the barbarian nomads of the future will encamp their mechanised caravans" (1948: 108). Moreover,

> To . . . aim to make everyone [the people he calls "the 'uneducated' mass of the population"] share in the appreciation of the fruits of the most conscious part of culture is to adulterate and cheapen what you give. For it is an essential condition of the preservation of the quality of the culture of the minority, that it should continue to be a minority culture. (106–7)

Eliot was also much more explicit about the role of social class in the functioning of culture. He maintains that one of the "important conditions [for] the hereditary transmission of culture [is] the persistence of social classes" (15). The class structure, class privilege, and class inequality are "essential conditions for the growth and for the survival of culture" (16). He tells his readers that if they "find it shocking that culture and equalitarianism should conflict, if it seems monstrous to him that anyone should have 'advantages of birth' – I do not ask him to change his faith, I merely ask him to stop paying lip-service to culture." He is very clear that "education should help to preserve the class and to select the elite" (100). As a result, he totally rejects what he calls "the Equality of Opportunity

26

dogma" (102). As he explains, in a claim which reeks of the need to establish cultural deference, "A high average of general education is perhaps less necessary for civil society than is a respect for learning" (100). With this in view, like both Arnold and the Leavisites he looks back longingly to a time when "people had the education necessary for the functions they were called upon to perform" (105). He totally rejects "the ideal of a uniform system [of education] such that no one capable of receiving higher education could fail to get it, [which] leads imperceptibly to the education of too many people, and consequently to the lowering of standards to whatever this swollen number of candidates is able to reach" (101).

The Marxist Masses

In 1947 Theodor Adorno and Max Horkheimer coined the term "culture industry" to describe the products and the processes of "mass culture." The cultural commodities produced by the culture industry, they claim, are marked by homogeneity: "film, radio and magazines make up a system which is uniform as a whole and in every part . . . all mass culture is identical" (1979: 120–1). As a consequence of homogeneity, the cultural commodities produced by the culture industry are always predictable:

> As soon as the film begins, it is quite clear how it will end, and who will be rewarded, punished, or forgotten. In light music [popular music], once the trained ear has heard the first notes of the hit song, it can guess what is coming and feel flattered when it does come . . . The result is a constant reproduction of the same thing. (125, 134)

Whereas Arnold, the Leavisites, and Ortega y Gasset had worried that popular culture as mass culture represented a threat to cultural and social authority, Adorno and Horkheimer argue that it actually produces the opposite effect; that is, it actually maintains social authority. Instead of "anarchy," they could see only dull "conformity": a situation in which "the deceived masses" (133) are caught in a "circle of manipulation and retroactive need in which the unity of the system grows ever stronger" (121). For example, "The sound film leaves no room for imagination or reflection on the part of the audience . . . they react automatically [and] fall helpless victims to what is offered them" (133–4). In the same way, listening to the radio "turns all participants into listeners and authoritatively subjects them to broadcast programmes which are all exactly the same, [producing] the stunting of the mass-media consumer's powers of imagination and spontaneity" (122).

The culture industry has depoliticized the working class – limited its horizon to political and economic goals that could be realized within the oppressive and exploitative framework of capitalist society. As Herbert Marcuse (1968: 26–7) claims in *One-Dimensional Man*:

> the irresistible outputs of the entertainment and information industry [the culture industry] carry with them prescribed attitudes and habits, certain intellectual and emotional reactions which bind the consumers more or less pleasantly to the producers and, through the latter, to the whole. The products indoctrinate and manipulate; they promote a false consciousness which is immune against its falsehood . . . it becomes a way of life. It is a good way of life – much better than before – and as a good way of life, it militates against qualitative change. Thus emerges a pattern of *one-dimensional thought and behaviour* in which ideas, aspirations, and objectives that, by their content, transcend the established universe of discourse and action are either repelled or reduced to terms of this universe.

The culture industry is "a means for fettering consciousness. It impedes the development of autonomous, independent individuals who judge and decide consciously for themselves" (92). The work of the culture industry is to arrest and imprison our cultural and polit-ical imaginations, thus making it increasingly impossible to think outside the prevailing structures of power. The monotonous repetition and predigested sameness of it all blunts our capacities to think beyond it. Its content reconciles us to a world without change. The more blunted our imaginations become, the more susceptible we become to the pernicious content of mass culture. We are trapped in a swirl-ing circle of diminishing humanity and deepening social control.

In other words, by supplying the means for the satisfaction of certain needs, capitalism is able to prevent the formation of more fundamental desires. The culture industry thus stunts the political imagination. This effect is compounded by the way in which work and leisure under capitalism form a compelling relationship: the effects of the culture industry are guaranteed by the nature of work; the work process secures the effects of the culture industry. The function of the culture industry is, ultimately, to organize leisure time in the same way as industrialization has organized work time. Work under capitalism stunts the senses; the culture industry continues the process: "The escape from everyday drudgery which the whole culture industry promises . . . [is a] paradise . . . [of] the same old drudgery . . . escape . . . [is] predesigned to lead back to the starting point. Pleasure promotes the resignation which it ought to help to forget" (Adorno and Horkheimer 1979: 142). In short, work leads to mass culture; mass culture leads back to work.[3]

The same disabling pessimism is the main feature of the disillu-sioned American Trotskyite Dwight Macdonald. In his widely quoted essay, "A Theory of Mass Culture" (first published in 1957), he claims that

> Mass Culture is imposed from above. It is fabricated by techni-cians hired by businessmen; its audience are passive consumers, their participation limited to the choice between buying and not buying. The Lords of kitsch, in short, exploit the cultural needs of the masses in order to make a profit and/or to maintain their class rule. (1998: 23)

29

According to Macdonald, "The eruption of the masses onto the political stage had [produced] . . . disastrous cultural results" (24). In an argument we have already encountered in discussions of Arnold, the Leavisites, and Ortega y Gasset, he claims that this "problem" has been compounded by the absence of "a clearly defined cultural elite" (24). Without a cultural elite, America is under threat from a Gresham's Law of culture: the bad will drive out the good; the result will be not just a homogeneous culture but a "homogenized culture . . . that threatens to engulf everything in its spreading ooze" (27), dispersing the cream from the top and turning the American people into infantile masses (29). His conclusions are pessimistic to say the least: "far from Mass Culture getting better, we will be lucky if it doesn't get worse" (35).

Ways of Seeing Other People as Masses

There is a curious unity in the understanding of popular culture as mass culture from both the political left and right. The Left sees the masses as manipulated and unable to play the revolutionary role that certain versions of Marxist analysis say they are destined to play. The Right sees the masses as a threat to social privileges and as potential polluters of the sacred sphere of culture. The perspectives developed by Arnold, Leavisism, Eliot, the Frankfurt School, and Macdonald condemn the same things, but for different reasons. Popular culture as mass culture is attacked because it threatens cultural standards and social authority, and/or because it depoliticizes the working class and thus maintains the iron grip of social authority: "obedience to the rhythm of the iron system. . . . the *absolute* power of capitalism" (Adorno and Horkheimer 1979: 120).

The influence of seeing popular culture as mass culture is very difficult to overestimate: for more than a century it was undoubtedly the dominant paradigm in cultural analysis. Indeed, it could be argued that it still forms a kind of repressed "common sense" in certain areas of British and American academic and nonacademic life. The principal problem is its working assumption that popular culture as mass culture always represents little more than an example of cultural decline and potential political disorder. Given this assumption, theoretical research and empirical investigation only ever confirm what they always expect to find. It looks down from the splendid heights of high culture to what it sees as the commercial wastelands of mass culture, seeking only confirmation of cultural decline or the need for regulation and social control.

3

Popular Culture as the "Other" of High Culture

Although the distinction between high and popular culture, organized by practices of aesthetic evaluation, is of recent origin, it is often presented as having been in existence since the beginnings of human history. It is not difficult, however, to demonstrate that high culture started to become a significant institutional space only in the second half of the nineteenth century. This was the result of two causes: the selective appropriation by elite social groups of aspects of what had been until then a shared public culture, and certain features in the development of the cultural movement we think of as modernism.

The Making of High Culture

Paul DiMaggio (1998: 454) argues that "The distinction between high and popular culture, in its American version, emerged in the period between 1850 and 1900 out of the efforts of urban elites to build organizational forms that, first, isolated high culture and, second, differentiated it from popular culture." With particular reference to Boston, DiMaggio argues that "To create an institutional high culture, Boston's upper class had to accomplish three concurrent, but analytically distinct, projects: entrepreneurship, classification, and framing" (456). By practices of classification they put into social circulation clearly defined boundaries between entertainment and art (the legitimation of these boundaries articulating social class to culture). Through framing they established a new method of cultural appropriation (the aesthetic mode of perception). But the main project, upon which the other projects depended for their success, was cultural entrepreneurship: the establishment of organizational forms that the Boston elite could govern and control.

The distinction between high and popular, DiMaggio argues, is dependent on an organizational distinction between nonprofit cultural institutions run by private individuals or boards of trustees and the commercial, profit-seeking, culture industries. In the case of Boston, the two key institutions were the Museum of Fine Arts (established in 1873) and the Boston Symphony Orchestra (established in 1881). These institutions provided solid and visible form to the ideal of high culture. Furthermore, as DiMaggio maintains,

> The alliance between class and culture that emerged was defined by, and thus inseparable from, its organizational mediation. As a consequence, the classification "high culture/popular culture" is comprehensible only in its dual sense as characterizing both ritual classification and the organizational systems that give that classification meaning. (471)

Both institutions were organized around, and worked to promote, "an aesthetic ideology that distinguished sharply between the nobility of art and the vulgarity of mere entertainment" (456). The sacralization of art that was institutionalized and classified in terms of its distinctness by the social elite of Boston thus produced definitions of both high culture and what it was isolated from, mere entertainment, that is, popular culture as the "other" of high culture.

Although, like other elites, the elite of Boston claimed to be creating institutions and cultural practices that would be of benefit to the community as a whole, it was quite clear that "they defined the community to include only the elite and the upper-middle classes" (460). Their success can be measured by the fact that by the end of the nineteenth century in the realms of art and music there was a profound social distinction and a clear institutional distance between what practices counted as, and the different audiences for, high culture and popular culture. Quite simply, the more the Boston elite monopolized control over art and music, the more firmly established became the barriers and the boundaries that marked these practices as the exclusive culture of both themselves and aspiring members of the middle class.

Lawrence W. Levine (1988) makes a similar argument with regard to the changing cultural value of the plays of William Shakespeare in nineteenth-century America. He first demonstrates how Shakespeare's work was an integral part of popular entertainment in the first half of the nineteenth century. He then details how, in the second half of the nineteenth century, elite social groups engaged in an active appropriation and redefinition of Shakespeare's work: it was moved from entertainment to education, and from plays to be performed before an inclusive audience to plays to be performed before an exclusive audience or, better still, plays to be read as poetry in quiet seclusion.

In American theaters from the middle of the eighteenth century, and especially in the first half of the nineteenth, Shakespeare was "the most widely performed dramatist" (16). In addition, Levine draws attention to the many burlesques and parodies of Shakespeare's work that appeared on the nineteenth-century American stage. For example, Ophelia would be told by Hamlet, "Get thee to a brewery"; the soliloquy, "To be or not to be" might be sung to the tune of "Three Blind Mice"; *Richard III*, the most popular Shakespeare play in nineteenth-century America, was often parodied as Bad Dicky (14). Given the size and heterogeneity of the audience that would have attended such performances, Levine concludes that "Shakespeare must have been well known throughout the society since people cannot parody what is not familiar." The following joke could only work with audiences who were familiar with Shakespeare's *Othello*:

34

When was Desdemona like a ship?
When she was Moored. (quoted in Levine 1988: 16)

From the perspective of what Shakespeare represents in the late twentieth century, it was initially difficult for Levine to think of Shakespeare as popular culture. As he explains, "It took a great deal of evidence to allow me to transcend my own cultural assumptions and accept the fact that Shakespeare actually *was* popular culture in nineteenth-century America" (4). The plays were performed frequently and in front of large audiences. Moreover, "Shakespeare was performed not merely alongside popular entertainment as an elite supplement to it; Shakespeare was performed as an integral part of it. Shakespeare *was* popular entertainment in nineteenth-century America" (21).[1]

In the second half of the nineteenth century, Shakespeare's position in American culture began to change. It was, as Levine explains, a movement from entertainment for the many to education and enlightenment for the few:

If Shakespeare had been an integral part of mainstream culture in the nineteenth century, in the twentieth he had become part of "polite" culture – an essential ingredient in a complex we call, significantly, "legitimate" theater. He had become the possession of the educated portions of society who disseminated his plays for the enlightenment of the average folk who were to swallow him not for their entertainment but for their education, as a respite from – not as a normal part of – their usual cultural diet. (31)

Shakespeare's plays were gradually removed from the theatrical world of acrobats and jugglers, burlesques and parodies, dancers and singers, and were instead relocated in theatres where the audience was no longer a heterogeneous mix of American society, but had been reduced in the main to middle-class ladies and gentlemen, concerned as much with strategies of social distinction as they were with gazing

35

aesthetically at what was happening on the stage. By the twentieth century, Shakespeare had been "*transformed* from a playwright for the general public into one for a specific audience. . . . from popular culture to polite culture, from entertainment to erudition, from the property of 'Everyman' to the possession of a more elite circle" (56). Writing in the *Atlantic Monthly* in 1884, Richard Grant White captures perfectly the changing status of Shakespeare in American culture. He identifies what he calls "Shakespeareanism," which is "a cult, a religion, with priests and professional incense-burners, who live . . . by his worship." Here was a "new literary religion" of "shrine-makers" dedicated to the idea "that the reading of Shakespeare is an art, and the editing of him a mystery" (quoted in Levine 1988: 70). Evidence of the priesthood is not difficult to find. Writing in 1882, A. A. Lipscomb declared with the confidence of the convert to Shakespeareanism, "Shakespeare off the stage is far superior to Shakespeare on the stage." He argued that without "rigid mechanical training" one would never get access to Shakespeare's "special worth." Lipscomb predicted with great accuracy that Shakespeare "is destined to become the Shakespeare of the college and university, and even more the Shakespeare of private and select culture. Nor will he ever be perfectly himself at home anywhere else." This was a destiny fully supported by many middle-class intellectuals. For example, writing in *Arena* in 1890, A. C. Wheeler argued that performing the plays "materializes Shakespeare, and in doing so vulgarizes him. Intellectual good taste outside of the theatre spiritualizes him" (quoted in Levine 1988: 73). Given the increasing spiritual weight that the dramas were required to bear, it was not too long before the disciples of Shakespeareanism began to doubt that the humble actor Shakespeare could really be the author of such "inspired" plays.

What happened to Shakespeare also happened to opera.[2] Before the nineteenth century opera had established itself as an integral part of a shared public culture both in Europe and the United States. The opera house was in fact the "first musical institution to open its doors to the general public" (Zelochow 1993: 261). The first opera house opened in Venice in 1637: it presented "commercial opera run for profit . . . offering the new, up-to-date entertainment to anyone who could afford a ticket" (Raynor 1972: 169). As Henry Raynor (1982) observes, "The Venetian audience consisted of all social classes" (171). Bernard Zelochow (1993: 262) argues that this remained the case throughout the next two centuries.

> By the late eighteenth century and in the nineteenth century the opera played a preeminent role in the cultural life of Europe. The opera was enjoyed and understood by a broad cross section of urban Europeans and Americans. The opera house became the meeting place of all social classes in society . . . The absence of the concept of a classical repertoire is an index of the popularity and vigor of opera as a mode of communication and entertainment.[3]

By the nineteenth century, then, opera was established as a widely available form of popular entertainment consumed by people of all social classes. For example, on returning to the United States in 1866 from England, where he had been American Consul, George Makepeace Towle noted how "Lucretia Borgia and Faust, The Barber of Seville and Don Giovanni are everywhere popular; you may hear their airs in the drawing room and concert halls, as well as whistled by the street boys and ground out on the hand organs" (quoted in Levine 1988: 99–100). It is perhaps significant that it was the circus entrepreneur P. T. Barnum who in 1852 organized, and successfully promoted, the first major concert tour across the US by the soprano – the so-called "Swedish Nightingale" – Jenny Lind (perhaps opera's first superstar).

To turn opera into "high culture" it had to be withdrawn from the everyday world of popular entertainment, especially from the heterogeneous dictates of the market and the commercial reach of cultural entrepreneurs. Bruce A. McConachie (1988) argues that between 1825 and 1850 elite social groups in New York developed three overlapping social strategies which gradually separated opera from the everyday world of popular entertainment. The first was to

37

separate it from theater by establishing buildings specifically for the performance of opera. Second, they

> also worked to sharpen and objectify a code of behavior, including a dress code, deemed proper when attending the opera. Finally, upper-class New Yorkers increasingly insisted that only foreign-language opera could meet their standards of excellence – standards upheld by behavior and criticism employing foreign words and specialized language impenetrable to all but the cognoscenti. (1988: 182)

As a consequence, "In 1825 theatre audiences from all classes enjoyed opera as a part of the social conventions of traditional playgoing behavior. By the Civil War [1861–5] the elite had excluded all but themselves and spectators from other classes willing to behave in ways deemed 'proper' according to upper-class norms."

Levine (1988: 102), however, maintains that it is only at the end of the nineteenth century that opera can be said to have been effectively isolated from other forms of entertainment. It is only then, he argues, that there begins to be a growing social acceptance of the "insistence that opera was a 'higher' form of art demanding a cultivated audience." For example, in 1900 the Metropolitan Opera, New York, had completed its season with a production of four acts from four different operas. This had been a common practice throughout most of the nineteenth century. But times were changing and music critic W. J. Henderson, writing in the *New York Times*, was quick to remind his readers of the new dispensation:

> There were people who had never heard "Carmen" before. There were people who had never heard of "Il Flauto Magico." There were people who had never heard "Lucia" . . . There were people who did not know any one of the three ladies in "The Magic Flute." This was an audience there only to hear "the famous singers." What they got was "a hotchpotch . . . of extracts . . . a program of broken candy."

In producing such a show, the Metropolitan Opera had, according to Henderson, removed "all semblance of art in the opera house" (quoted in Levine 1988: 103).

Henderson's words no longer signaled a threatened elitism, as they might have done 50 years earlier. On the contrary, Henderson was articulating what would become the commonplace attitude of the culture of twentieth-century opera, that is, opera was no longer a form of living entertainment, it was increasingly a source of "Culture" with a capital C – a resource of both aesthetic enlightenment and social validation. The success of this invention can be heard in Oscar Hammerstein's confident claim (made in 1910) that

> grand opera [is] . . . the most elevating influence upon modern society, after religion. From the earliest days it has ever been the most elegant of all forms of entertainment . . . it employs and unifies all the arts . . . I sincerely believe that nothing will make better citizenship than familiarity with grand opera. It lifts one so out of the sordid affairs of life and makes material things seem so petty, so inconsequential, that it places one for the time being, at least, in a higher and better world . . . Grand opera . . . is the awakening of the soul to the sublime and the divine. (quoted in DiMaggio 1992: 35)

DiMaggio (1992: 49) differs from both Levine and McConachie in his insistence that although there is clearly a "shift in opera's social constituency during the nineteenth century . . . issues of opera's definition, sponsorship, merit, and legitimacy were [not] resolved by the turn of the century." He argues that it is only in the 1930s, when opera adopts "the non-profit educational form" ("trustee-governed nonprofit organizations"), that opera's "legitimacy" as high culture is finally secured (40, 37). He cites the head of classical repertoire at RCA Victor, who wrote in 1936: "While in former years [opera] generally attracted large audiences primarily as a form of entertainment, today opera is commanding the attention of both

39

layman and serious musician as an important and significant art form" (quoted in DiMaggio 1992: 37).

Opera as "high culture" is therefore not a universal given, unfolding from its moment of intellectual birth; it is an historically specific category institutionalized (depending on which cultural historian you find most convincing) by the 1860s, 1900s, or 1930s. Although these accounts may differ in terms of periodization, what each demonstrates is how elite social groups in the major American cities began the process of constructing a separate social space in which opera could be self-evidently high culture. Similarly, as Janet Wolff (1989: 5–6) argues,

> A parallel process of differentiation had also been occurring in England, where the pre-industrial cultural pursuits, enjoyed on a cross-class basis, were gradually replaced by a class-specific culture, the high arts of music, theatre and literature being the province of the upper-middle and middle classes, and the popular cultural forms of music hall, organised sport and popular literature providing the entertainment of the lower classes.

Art, music, opera, and Shakespeare were removed from a shared public culture. Once rehoused in the temples of art, which the art museums, concert halls, opera houses, and "legitimate" theaters increasingly resembled, they became available as the special property of those with the social and economic power, the leisure time, and the education to appreciate Culture. As Levine (1988: 229) explains,

> What was invented in the late nineteenth century were the rituals accompanying th[e] appreciation [of high culture]; what was invented was the illusion that the aesthetic products of high culture were originally created to be appreciated in precisely the manner late nineteenth-century Americans were taught to observe: with reverent, informed, disciplined seriousness.

What was put in place – at times uneasily – was not just a new culture and a new cultural divide between (high) culture and mass culture, but a sense of cultural authority in which culture is better than mass culture, and perhaps more important, that those who consume culture are superior to those who consume mass culture.[4]

The Modernist Revolution

The selective appropriation by social elites of aspects of what had been until then a shared public culture was paralleled by the cultural strategies of many of the artists and theorists of the cultural movement we now call modernism. As John Carey (1992: 1) argues,

> modernist literature and art can be seen as a hostile reaction to the unprecedentedly large reading public created by late nineteenth-century educational reforms. The purpose of modernist writing . . . was to exclude these newly educated (or "semi-educated") readers, and so to preserve the intellectual's seclusion from the "mass."

Moreover, "the principle around which modernist literature and culture fashioned themselves was the exclusion of the masses, the defeat of their power, the removal of their literacy, the denial of their humanity" (21). Andreas Huyssen (1986: vii) makes much the same point,

> Ever since the mid-19th century, the culture of modernity has been characterized by a volatile relationship between high art and mass culture . . . Modernism constituted itself through a conscious strategy of exclusion, an anxiety of contamination by its other: an increasingly consuming and engulfing mass culture.

According to modernist art critic Clement Greenberg, in the mid-nineteenth century the arts began to pursue a particular strategy

41

in order to avoid incorporation into the newly emerging culture industries: "The arts could save themselves from this levelling down only by demonstrating that the kind of experience they provided was valuable in its own right and not to be obtained from any other activity" (74). To successfully escape the culture industries, art had to supposedly "purify" itself. Instead of representations of reality, it turned to representations of itself. Rather than use "art to conceal art," it "used art to call attention to art" (Greenberg 1965: 194). "From painting things, the painter has turned to painting ideas" (Ortega y Gasset 1968: 38).

A key aspect of this process of purification was the necessity to establish minority against majority in matters of culture. Ortega y Gasset (writing in 1948), for example, is very explicit about the necessary course of action: "All modern art is unpopular, and it is so not accidentally and by chance, but essentially and by fate" (1968: 4). This is because modern art is "antipopular": it is "a social agent which . . . divides the public into the two classes of those who understand it ['a specially gifted minority'] and those who do not ['the shapeless mass of the many']" (5–6). In this way, then, "the new art also helps the elite to recognize themselves and one another in the drab mass of society and to learn their mission which consists in being few and holding their own against the many" (7). Furthermore, the new art will expose "the provoking and profound injustice of the assumption that men are actually equal."

Modernism's self-image – an exclusive and excluding cultural practice – disguises the fact that modernism's autonomy as a cultural practice (freed from the interference of the church and the stifling embrace of patronage) is dependent on the very market economy it pretends to despise. Like the culture industries it defines itself against, modernist high culture owes its very existence to the success of the capitalist market economy. As Huyssen (1986: 17) so rightly observes, "The irony of course is that art's aspirations to autonomy, its uncoupling from church and state, became possible only when literature, painting and music were first organised according to the principles of a market economy."

42

The Politics of Cultural Exclusion

The work of the French sociologist Pierre Bourdieu (1984, 1993) offers a very profitable way to understand the making of cultural exclusivity in the late nineteenth and early twentieth centuries. Bourdieu's work helps to explain two things: first, how the power of social class operates across the field of culture; and second, how actions in the field of culture help reproduce the inequalities of social class. He argues that social practices of cultural consumption, which involve the making, marking, and maintaining of social difference, help to secure and legitimate forms of power and domination which are rooted in economic inequality. In other words, he argues that although class rule is ultimately economic, the form it takes is cultural. The source of social difference and social power is thus symbolically shifted from the economic field to the field of cultural consumption, making social power appear to be the result of a specific cultural disposition. In this way, the production and reproduction of cultural space helps to produce and reproduce social space, social power, and class difference.

Bourdieu is interested not so much in the actual differences, but in how these differences are used by dominant classes as a means of social reproduction. He argues, therefore, that what people consume does not simply reflect distinctions and differences embedded elsewhere, which cultural consumption makes visible, but that cultural consumption is the means by which they are produced, maintained, and reproduced. He seeks to demonstrate how what social groups consume is part of a strategy for making a hierarchy of social space. He shows how arbitrary tastes and arbitrary ways of living are continually transmuted into legitimate taste and the only legitimate way of life. As he points out, "taste classifies, and it classifies the classifier" (1984: 6). We are classified by our classifications and classify others by theirs. While such strategies of classification do not in themselves produce social inequalities, the making, marking, and maintaining of them functions to legitimate such inequalities. In this

43

way, taste is a profoundly ideological discourse; it functions as a marker of "class" (using the term in the double sense to mean both socio-economic category and a particular level of quality). Although culture does not produce or cause class divisions and inequalities, "cultural consumption [is] predisposed . . . to fulfil a social function of legitimating social difference" (7).

In order to successfully make what is cultural appear as a gift of nature, it is essential to deny (consciously and unconsciously) the link between art appropriation and "education" (both the formal kind and that informally found within the family setting). This process of denial produces and internalizes what Bourdieu calls the "cultivated disposition" (230). As he explains (1993: 234),

> members of the privileged classes are naturally inclined to regard as a gift of nature a cultural heritage which is transmitted by a process of unconscious training . . . Culture is thus achieved only by negating itself as such, that is, as artificial and artificially acquired, so as to become second nature, a habitus, a possession turned into being.

Being in denial allows one to be in power:

> silence concerning the social prerequisites for the appropriation of culture or, to be more exact, for the acquisition of art competence in the sense of mastery of all the means for the specific appropriation of works of art is a self-seeking silence because it is what makes it possible to legitimise a social privilege by pretending that it is a gift of nature.

Against this denial, Bourdieu reminds us that "culture is not what one is but what one has, or rather, what one has become."

In this way, then, "the privileged members of bourgeois society replace the difference between two cultures [middle-class and working-class], historic products of social conditions, by the essential difference between two natures, a naturally cultivated nature and a

44

naturally natural nature" (1993: 236). The "illusion of 'natural distinction' is ultimately based on the power of the dominant to impose, by their very existence, a definition of excellence which [is] nothing other than their own way of existing" (1984: 255). A hierarchy of taste is mapped onto a hierarchy of social class and the former is used to legitimate the latter. According to Bourdieu, then, "the function of culture . . . is to strengthen the feeling of belonging in some and the feeling of exclusion in others" (1993: 236).[5]

Culture and Class

I do not claim that before the making of cultural exclusivity in the late nineteenth and early twentieth centuries there had not previously existed a visible connection between cultural taste and social class. But what had changed – and this is what I mean by the invention of popular culture as the "other" of high culture – was the institutionalization of this connection between class and culture. Removing, for example, opera and Shakespeare, from the heterogeneous demands of the market ensured that differences in taste could be marked by, and be indicative of, clear social boundaries. As DiMaggio (1992: 22) makes clear:

> as long as cultural boundaries were indistinct, "fashionable taste," far from embodying cultural authority, was suspect as snobbish, trivial, and undemocratic. Only when elite taste was harnessed to a clearly articulated ideology embodied in the exhibitions and performances of organizations that selected and presented art in a manner distinct from that of commercial entrepreneurs . . . did an understanding of culture as hierarchical become both legitimate and widespread.

Therefore, to turn opera and Shakespeare into "high culture" they had to be withdrawn from the everyday world of popular entertainment. It is important to realize that opera and Shakespeare did not become unpopular; rather, they were *made* unpopular. That is, they were actively appropriated from their popular audience by elite social groups determined to situate them as the crowning glory of their culture (so-called "high culture"). In short, opera and Shakespeare were transformed from entertainment enjoyed by the many into Culture to be appreciated by the few.

American sociologist Richard Peterson (1992) argues that the distinction between elite and popular culture is beginning to give way to a difference between "omnivorous" and "univorous" patterns of consumption. Distinction created by consumption is no longer secured by restricting consumption to forms of high culture; distinction is now to be had by knowing about and participating in a wide repertoire of cultural practices.

The elite-to-mass model assumes a hierarchy in which the dominant social class has a well-defined pattern of consumption in terms of what, how, and where to consume, together with an attitude of contempt for mass culture and those for whom mass culture is culture. What is changing is this: rather than consume only high culture, members of the dominant class now also consume much of what they had previously dismissed as mass culture. For example, when "high-status groups," those who in the late nineteenth and early twentieth centuries would have been actively engaged in the appropriation of opera from its popular audience, were asked to name their favourite music, country music scored 9 percent, while opera scored only 6 percent. Although 30 percent named classical music as their favorite, 13.3 percent said they could not limit their choice to just one type of music (Peterson 1992: 248; Peterson and Simkus 1992: 169). Distinction, however, remains, but the strategies for securing distinction are changing. Put simply, what matters is not what you consume but how you consume it. This does not mean that "the US is becoming a more egalitarian society, [nor] does it mean that leisure activities and taste in music are losing their efficacy as status markers for the elite . . . It may just mean that the image of the taste-*exclusive* highbrow, along with ranking from 'snob' to 'slob,' is obsolete" (Peterson 1992: 252).

Figure 3.1 Cultural consumption and social class.

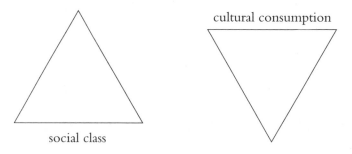

Peterson suggests that we can visualize his argument as two pyramids overlaying each other (see figure 3.1). One right side up, representing a hierarchy of social class, and the other upside down, representing omnivore-to-univore taste cultures.

The symbolic boundaries of taste still exist, as do the social hierarchies they support and make visible, but they are increasingly no longer based on cultural exclusivity but on a very particular mode of cultural appropriation, which is both intellectual and intertextual. In a development which offers a curious parallel to the emergence of opera "homework" books (discussed in chapter 5), elite magazines and journals have begun to discuss country music with a level of seriousness once reserved only for classical music and opera; such essays and articles "provide omnivores with the tools they need to develop an aesthetic understanding of country music" (Peterson and Kern 1996: 904).

4

Popular Culture as an Arena of Hegemony

How I think about the relations between culture and power is informed primarily by the work of the Italian Marxist Antonio Gramsci (1971, 1998). Although it is true that since the introduction of Gramsci's work into cultural studies in the 1970s, cultural studies has been influenced by (and has in turn influenced) feminism, post-structuralism, post-colonial theory, psychoanalysis, postmodernism, and queer theory, I would argue that the work of Gramsci is still fundamental to cultural studies, certainly as it is practiced in the UK.

Hegemony: From Marxism to Cultural Studies

Hegemony is for Gramsci a political concept developed to explain the absence of socialist revolutions in the capitalist democracies. The concept is used by Gramsci to refer to a *condition in process* in which a dominant class (in alliance with other classes or class fractions) does not merely *rule* a society but *leads* it through the exercise of "moral and intellectual leadership" (Gramsci 1998: 210). This produces a situation in which the interests of one powerful section of society are "universalized" as the interests of the society as a whole. In this sense, hegemony is used to suggest a society in which, despite oppression and exploitation, there is a high degree of "consensus"; a society in which subordinate groups and classes appear to actively support and subscribe to values, ideals, objectives, cultural and political meanings, which "incorporate" them into the prevailing structures of power.[1]

Although hegemony implies a society with a high degree of consensus, it should not be understood to refer to a society in which all conflict has been removed. What the concept is meant to suggest is a society in which conflict is contained and managed. That is, hegemony is maintained (and must be continually maintained: it is an ongoing process) by dominant groups and classes "negotiating" with, and making concessions to, subordinate groups and classes. For example, consider the historical case of British hegemony in the Caribbean. One of the ways in which Britain attempted to secure its control over the indigenous population, and the African men, women, and children it had transported there as slaves, was by means of the imposition of a version of British culture (a standard practice for colonial regimes everywhere): part of the process was to institute English as the official language. In linguistic terms, the result was not the imposition of English but, for the majority of the population, the creation of a new language. The dominant element of this new language is English, but the language itself is not simply English. What emerged was a transformed English, with new stresses, new rhythms, and new meanings, with some words dropped and new words introduced (from African languages and elsewhere). The new language was the result of a "negotiation" between dominant and subordinate cultures, that is, not a language imposed from above nor a language which spontaneously had arisen from below, but a language that was the result of a hegemonic struggle between two language cultures, a dominant language culture and a subordinate language culture, involving both "resistance" and "incorporation." Hegemony, therefore, is not domination from above in the sense implied by the term "dominant ideology," in which any notion of struggle is squeezed to nothing under the deadening weight of imposition from above. Nor is hegemony another word for liberal

49

consensus, in which different positions circulate in equal plurality. Hegemony is a particular kind of consensus, one in which there is an active and ongoing struggle to win support, through strategies of "moral and intellectual leadership," for the continued rule of the dominant class.

Hegemony is "organized" by those whom Gramsci designates "organic intellectuals," According to Gramsci, intellectuals are distinguished by their social function. That is to say, all men and women have the capacity for intellectual activity, but only certain men and women in society have the function of intellectuals. Each class, as Gramsci explains, creates "organically" its own intellectuals. Organic intellectuals function as class organizers (in the broadest sense of both terms). They give a class

> homogeneity and an awareness of its own function not only in the economic sphere but also in the social and political fields. The capitalist entrepreneur [for example] creates alongside himself the industrial technician, the specialist in political economy, the organisers of a new culture, of a new legal system, etc. (212)

It is the task of the organic intellectuals of the dominant class to "determine and to organise the reform of moral and intellectual life" (210). They are, in short, the dominant class's "deputies," striving to secure and sustain its hegemony. I have argued elsewhere (Storey 1985) that Matthew Arnold is an organic intellectual, what Gramsci identifies as one of "an elite of men of culture, who have the function of providing leadership of a cultural and general ideological nature" (quoted in Storey 1985: 149–50). Gramsci tends to speak of organic intellectuals as individuals, but the way the concept has been mobilized in cultural studies, following Louis Althusser's (1998) barely acknowledged borrowings from Gramsci, is in terms of *collective* organic intellectuals – the so-called "ideological state apparatuses," which include the family, television, the press, education, organized religion, the culture industries, etc.[2]

The introduction of Gramsci's concept of hegemony into British cultural studies in the early 1970s brought about a rethinking of popular culture. It did this in two ways. First of all it produced a rethinking of the politics of popular culture: popular culture was now seen as a key site for the production and reproduction of hegemony. Capitalist industrial societies are societies divided unequally in terms of, for example, "race," ethnicity, gender, generation, sexuality, and social class. Popular culture is one of the principal sites where these divisions are established and contested; that is, popular culture is an arena of struggle and negotiation between the interests of dominant groups and the interests of subordinate groups.

The introduction of hegemony into British cultural studies also produced a rethinking of the concept of popular culture itself (Hall 1996b, Storey 2001). This rethinking involved bringing into active relationship two previously dominant but antagonistic ways of thinking about popular culture. The first tradition viewed popular culture as a culture imposed by the capitalist culture industries, a culture provided for profit and ideological manipulation. This is popular culture as "structure." The second tradition saw popular culture as a culture spontaneously emerging from below; an "authentic" folk culture, working-class culture, or subculture – the "voice" of the people. This is popular culture as "agency." From the perspective of Gramscian cultural studies, however, popular culture is neither an "authentic" folk culture, working-class culture, or subculture, nor a culture simply imposed by the capitalist culture industries, but a "compromise equilibrium" (Gramsci 1998: 211) between the two – a contradictory mix of forces from both "below" and "above," both "commercial" and "authentic," marked by both "resistance" and "incorporation," "structure" and "agency." Therefore, although a primary interest for cultural studies is the investigation of how people make culture from and with the commodities made available by the capitalist culture industries, working with the concept of hegemony is to insist that such research should never lose sight of the conditions of existence which both enable and constrain practices of cultural production and consumption.

51

From the perspective of hegemony theory, the cultural field is marked by a struggle to articulate, disarticulate, and rearticulate cultural texts and practices for particular ideologies, particular politics. As Stuart Hall (1985: 34) points out, "Meaning is a social production, a practice. The world has to be *made to mean*." Therefore, because different meanings can be ascribed to the same cultural text, practice, or event, meaning is always the site and the result of struggle.[3] A key question for cultural studies is: "Why do particular meanings get regularly constructed around, say, particular cultural practices and thereby achieve the status of 'common sense,' acquire a certain taken-for-granted quality?" Although this is a recognition that the culture industries are a major site of ideological production, constructing powerful images, descriptions, definitions, frames of reference for understanding the world, Gramscian cultural studies rejects the view that "the people" who consume these productions are "cultural dupes," victims of "an up-dated form of the opium of the people." As Hall (1998: 446) insists,

> That judgement may make us feel right, decent and self-satisfied about our denunciations of the agents of mass manipulation and deception – the capitalist cultural industries: but I don't know that it is a view which can survive for long as an adequate account of cultural relationships; and even less as a socialist perspective on the culture and nature of the working class. Ultimately, the notion of the people as a purely passive, outline force is a deeply unsocialist perspective.

Gramscian cultural studies is informed by the proposition that people *make* popular culture from the repertoire of commodities supplied by the culture industries. *Making* popular culture ("production in use") can be empowering to subordinate and resistant to dominant understandings of the world. But this is not to say that popular culture is always empowering and resistant. To deny the passivity of consumption is not to deny that sometimes consumption is passive; to deny that the consumers of popular culture are cultural dupes is

52

not to deny that the culture industries seek to manipulate. But it is to deny that popular culture is little more than a degraded landscape of commercial and ideological manipulation, imposed from above in order to make profit and secure social control. Gramscian cultural studies insists that to decide these matters requires vigilance and attention to the details of the production, distribution, and consumption of the commodities from which people may or may not make culture (Storey 1999). These are not matters that can be decided once and for all (outside the contingencies of history and politics) with an elitist glance and a condescending sneer. Nor can they be read off from the moment of production (locating meaning, pleasure, ideological effect, the probability of incorporation, the possibility of resistance in, variously, the intention, the means of production, or the production itself). These are only aspects of the contexts for "production in use"; and it is, ultimately, in "production in use" that questions of meaning, pleasure, ideological effect, incorporation, or resistance can be (contingently) decided.

Wandering from the Path of Righteousness

From the perspective of political economy, the deployment of hegemony in cultural studies is seen as inevitably leading to an uncritical focus on questions of consumption (see Garnham 1998). More specifically, it is said that work on consumption in cultural studies has vastly overestimated the power of consumers by failing to keep in view the "determining" role of production. What this seems to mean is that cultural studies should stop being cultural studies and become instead political economy. So what has political economy got to offer? According to Peter Golding and Graham Murdock (1991: 15), political economy "sets out to show how different ways of financing and organising cultural production have traceable consequences for the range of discourses and representations in the public domain and for audiences' *access to* them" (my italics). The significant word here is "access" (privileged over "appropriation,"

53

"use," or "meaning"). Political economy's idea of cultural analysis seems to involve little more than detailing access to, and availability of, cultural commodities and commodified practices. Nowhere do they actually advocate a consideration of what these commodities might mean (textually) or be made to mean in use (consumption). As Golding and Murdock point out, "political economy seeks to relate variations in people's responses to their overall location in the economic system" (27).

Similarly, Ferguson and Golding (1997: xxiv) claim that "the shaping and packaging of most urban popular culture today results from sophisticated celebrity and product marketing on the part of media organisations before any element of consumer choice enters the marketplace." Now even if this is true, it is only the beginning of the process that is better understood, to borrow Stuart Hall's (1996d: 45) phrase, as "determination by the economic in the *first* instance." "Access" is the end of one process ("production") and the beginning of another ("consumption"). Moreover, as Gramsci (1971: 184), in a slightly different context, observed,

> It may be ruled out that immediate economic crises of themselves produce fundamental historical events; they can simply create a terrain more favourable to the dissemination of certain modes of thought, and certain ways of posing and resolving questions involving the entire subsequent development of national life.

In other words, we will not understand the relations between culture and power by pretending that all the answers can be found in an analysis of the conditions of existence or by making a fetish of the "determining" role of production. However, we will not understand the relations between culture and power by pretending that conditions of existence are unimportant; it is the relationship between the two that needs to be adequately understood. While it is clearly important to locate the commodities people consume within the field of the economic conditions of their existence, it is clearly insufficient to do this and think you have also already analyzed important questions of appropriation, meaning, and use. Therefore, what is needed is *not just* an understanding of how production produces a repertoire of commodities for consumption, but *also* an understanding of the many ways in which people appropriate, make meaningful, and use these commodities, *make them into culture* in the lived practices of everyday life. Michael Denning (1987: 26), in a discussion of the production of dime novels as a part of the emerging culture industries in nineteenth-century America, makes the point that

> As in other capitalist industries, there are struggles both at the point of production, the writing of these dime novels; and at the point of consumption, the reading of cheap stories. So a history of dime novels is not simply a history of a culture industry; it also encompasses a history of their place in working class culture, and of their role in the struggles to reform that culture.

In other words, analysis must take seriously questions of both structure and agency. The trouble with much of the work of political economy is that it encourages a detailed understanding of the workings of production, while suggesting that a cursory glance will be more than enough to understand the practices of cultural consumption.

Political economy is very good at reminding cultural studies that consumption is not something freely available to all; that there exist real inequalities (in terms of resources and education), which exclude many people from exercising their "sovereign" power in the market. And although political economy has undoubtedly made a major contribution to showing how cultures are structured unequally in terms of concentration of ownership and authority, production of repertoires, unequal access to cultural goods, political economy has remained reluctant to examine how people operate within these structures. Too often, political economy's idea of cultural anaysis involves little more than detailing access to or availability of

55

commodities. Rarely do they actually advocate a consideration of the specific materiality of these commodities (textual analysis) or how these commodities are made to mean in actual use (practices of consumption). They seem happy instead to suggest that audience negotiations are fictions, merely illusory moves in a game of economic power. I think, however, that it is important to distinguish between the power of the culture industries and the power of their influence. Too often the two are conflated, but they are not necessarily the same. The trouble with political economy is that too often it is assumed that they are the same. To explore the extent of the influence of the culture industries requires specific and detailed focus on consumption as it is actually lived and practiced in particular social contexts, and not as it *should* be experienced as *already determined* in a prior analysis of the relations of production or the economic conditions of existence. There is a real sense in which the insistence on production as the only really valid object of study is really a rejection of "agency." As Angela McRobbie (1996: 252) observes,

> It is as though "letting the people in" to the field of analysis rocks the boat of left consensus. The people are too difficult in their diversity, too unpredictable in their tastes, too likely to stray from the path of class politics, that it is better and perhaps safer to run the risk of being seen as elitist and have them safely suffering from either "false consciousness" or ideological seduction.

Side Saddle on the Golden Calf

Paul Willis (1990) argues that the capitalist drive for profit produces contradictions in the market, "supplying materials for its own critique" (19). As he explains, "People find on the market incentives and possibilities not simply for their own confinement but also for their own development and growth" (27). It is crude and simplistic to assume that the effects of consumption must mirror the intentions of production. The capitalist commodity has a double existence, as both use value and exchange value. Use value refers to "the ability of the commodity to satisfy some human want" (Lovell 1998: 476). Such wants, says Marx, "may spring from the stomach or from the fancy" (quoted in Lovell 1998: 476). As Lovell (1998: 477) observes, "the use value of a commodity cannot be known in advance of investigation of actual use of the commodity."

The primary concern of capitalist production is exchange value leading to surplus value (i.e. profit). This does not mean, of course, that capitalism is uninterested in use value: without use value commodities would not sell. But it does mean that the individual capitalist's search for surplus value can often be at the expense of what might be the general ideological needs of the system as a whole. Marx was more aware than most of the contradictions in the capitalist system. Discussing bourgeois demands that workers should save in order better to endure the fluctuations of boom and slump, Marx (1976: 287) pointed to the tension which exists between "worker as producer" and "worker as consumer":

each capitalist does demand that his workers should save, but only *his* own, because they stand towards him as workers; but by no means the remaining *world of workers*, for these stand towards him as consumers. In spite of all "pious" speeches he therefore searches for means to spur them on to consumption.

Sometimes it is not the complexities and contradictions of capitalism that have been ignored, but capitalism itself. Hall (1996c) is probably right to suggest that many working in cultural studies have not just rejected "economic determinism," but have, in fear of reductionism, turned away entirely from economic explanations. As a consequence, rather than produce alternative ways of thinking about the economic conditions of existence, there has been rather "a massive, gigantic, and eloquent *disavowal*. As if, since the economic in the broadest sense, definitely does *not*, as it was once supposed to

57

do, 'determine' the real movement of history 'in the last instance', it does not exist at all!'" (258). Acknowledging this, however, does not point to the need to build bridges to political economy. The problem with political economy, as Hall (1996b: 47) points out, is that "It tends to conceive the economic level as not only a 'necessary' but a 'sufficient' explanation of cultural and ideological effects." What is required is not a falling down before the "eternal verities of political economy" (Morley 1997: 121) but a renewed commitment to a Gramscian cultural studies.

Taking seriously the "economic," however, should not mean abandoning work on consumption. There are two reason why I think cultural studies should continue (regardless of the criticisms of political economy) to examine practices of consumption. The first is a theoretical reason: to know how commodities are used and made to mean requires a consideration of consumption. This will take us beyond an interest in the meaning of a commodity (that is, meaning as something "essential," inscribed and guaranteed), to a focus on the range of meanings that a commodity makes possible (that is, its "social" meanings, how it is appropriated and used in practices of consumption). This point is often missed in critiques of ethnography and audience studies. Cultural studies work on consumption is not a means to verify the "true" meaning or meanings of a commodity (or a commodified practice). Rather, investigation is undertaken as a means to discover the meanings people make, the meanings which circulate and become embedded in the lived cultures of people's everyday lives. Working on consumption may lead at times to a certain celebration of the lived cultures of "ordinary" people, but such celebration is usually made in the full knowledge that what in one context is "resistance" can become in another "incorporation."

The second reason I think cultural studies should continue to be concerned with consumption is political. Cultural studies, as I pointed out in the preface, is a "democratic" project in the sense that rather than studying only what Matthew Arnold called "the best which has been thought and said," cultural studies is committed (in principle if not in practice) to examining *all* that has been thought and said. For this reason I think it should reject the "pessimistic elitism" which haunts so much work in cultural theory and analysis, which routinely discounts the experiences of "ordinary" people, and always seems to want to suggest that "agency" is always overwhelmed by "structure" and that consumption is a mere shadow of production. Moreover, "pessimistic elitism" is a way of thinking which seeks to present itself as a form of radical cultural politics. But too often this is a politics in which attacks on power end up being little more than self-serving revelations about how "other people" (the "masses") are always "cultural dupes."[4]

Although, as I said earlier, cultural studies recognizes that the capitalist culture industries are a major site of ideological production, constructing powerful images, descriptions, definitions, frames of reference for understanding the world, it must continue to insist on the active complexity, and situated agency, of consumption. Culture is not something ready-made which we "consume"; culture is what we *make* in the varied practices of consumption. This distinction is there at the very beginning of British cultural studies. Richard Hoggart (writing in 1957), for example, observes that

> Songs which do not meet the requirements [of working-class people] are not likely to be taken up, no matter how much Tin Pan Alley plugs them . . . [P]eople do not have to sing or listen to these songs, and many do not: and those who do, often make the songs better than they really are . . . [P]eople often read them in their own way. So that even there they are less affected than the extent of their purchases would seem to indicate. (1990: 231)

Similarly, Raymond Williams (1958b: 425) rejects what he calls

> the extremely damaging and quite untrue identification of "popular culture" . . . with "working-class culture". In fact the main source of this "popular culture" lies outside the working

class altogether, for it is instituted, financed and operated by the commercial bourgeoisie, and remains typically capitalist in its methods of production and distribution. That working-class people form perhaps a majority of the consumers of this material . . . does not, as a fact, justify this facile identification.

The truth is that cultural studies has never rejected the need to analyze production. What was rejected were reductive and reflectionist modes of analysis, which focused solely on the mode of production and viewed consumption as the unproblematic mirror of production; clouded only occasionally by the ineffectual activities of consumers performing their role as "cultural dupes." There is no hidden logic in cultural studies which makes it inevitable that it must turn its back on production or, more importantly, the relations between production and consumption. For example, Hall's 1970s model of encoding and decoding, with its circuit of production, distribution, and consumption (Hall 1980); Richard Johnson's 1980s model of production, texts, readings, and lived cultures (1996); the Open University's 1990s circuit of culture, consisting of the processes of production, consumption, regulation, representation, identity (Du Gay et al. 1997). Each in its different way has sought to keep production (structural forms) and consumption (forms of agency) in an active and critical relationship. All draw on Marx's understanding of structure and agency: "Men [and women] make their own history, but they do not make it just as they please; they do not make it under circumstances chosen by themselves, but under circumstances directly encountered, given and transmitted from the past" (1977: 10).

We make history and we are made by history; we make culture and we are made by culture. Culture (like language) both enables and constrains. In the 1950s it was formulated by Hoggart (1990: 19) as "Against this background may be seen how much the more generally diffused appeals of the mass publications connect with commonly accepted attitudes, how they are altering those attitudes and how they are meeting resistance." In the 1960s it is given a

60

culturalist accent in Hall and Whannel's (1964: 280) observation that "Teenage culture is a contradictory mixture of the authentic and the manufactured: it is an area of self-expression for the young and a lush grazing pasture for the commercial providers." In the 1970s it was found in the Gramscian tones of John Clarke and others (1976: 11): "Men and women are . . . formed, and form themselves through society, culture and history . . . Each group makes something of its starting conditions – and through this 'making,' through this practice, culture is reproduced and transmitted." In the 1980s we hear it in the Foucauldian analysis of Mica Nava (1987: 209–10): "Consumerism is far more than just economic activity: it is also about dreams and consolation, communication and confrontation, image and identity . . . Consumerism is a discourse through which disciplinary power is both exercised and contested." In the 1990s it is there in Marie Gillespie's (1995: 2, 3) account of the relations between popular media and the consumption practices of migrant and diasporic communities, in which she demonstrates how young Punjabi Londoners are "shaped by but at the same time reshaping the images and meanings circulated in the media" – what she calls "re-creative consumption." In every decade in the history of cultural studies the point has been made and repeated. It is the "Gramscian insistence" (before, with, and after Gramsci), learned from Marx, that we make culture and we are made by culture; there is agency and there is structure. It is not enough to celebrate agency; nor is it enough to detail the structure(s) of power. We must always keep in mind the dialectical play between resistance and incorporation. The best of cultural studies has always been mindful of this.

An Inclusive Cultural Studies

What is needed is a more inclusive, a more tolerant cultural studies, one in which political economy and ethnography and audience studies can see themselves as contributing to the same project, existing like two sides of the same sheet of paper, differently inscribed but inescapably bound together in a project of understanding and dismantling the relations between culture and power. However, to establish a unity around "real" politics (as defined by political economy) seems to require cultural studies to dump feminism, discourse theory, queer theory, work on ethnicity and "race," and to return instead to a primary moment of pure class oppression, uncomplicated by sexuality, gender, ethnicity, or "race." I do not think this is going to happen (nor would I wish it to happen). As Judith Butler (1998: 44) has observed, talking more generally about political alliances on the Left,

> the tactical manipulation of the distinction between cultural and economic to reinstate the discredited notion of secondary oppression will only reprovoke the resistance to the imposition of unity, strengthening the suspicion that unity is only purchased through violent excision . . . This refusal to become resubordinated to a unity that caricatures, demeans, and domesticates difference becomes the basis for a more expansive and dynamic political impulse. This resistance to "unity" carries with it the cipher of democratic promise on the Left.

In the spirit of Butler's hope for an expansive and inclusive democratic politics of the Left, I would like to end this chapter by inviting those who identify their work as political economy to join (in critical harmony) with an inclusive and tolerant cultural studies, in the intellectual and academic project of rooting out and challenging the various and complex relations between culture and power.

5

Popular Culture as Postmodern Culture

The New Sensibility

In the 1960s Susan Sontag coined the term "new sensibility" to describe what she called the abandonment of "the Matthew Arnold notion of culture." She claimed that the Arnoldian idea of culture was, "historically and humanly obsolescent," adding that "the distinction between 'high' and 'low' culture seems less and less meaningful" (Sontag 1966: 296, 299, 302). Evidence of the new sensibility can be seen in the cultural valorization of the music of popular performers like Bob Dylan and the Beatles. Perhaps a more obvious example is the Pop Art movement of the 1960s, which was founded on a rejection of the distinction between popular and high culture. As Pop Art's first theorist, Lawrence Alloway, explains,

> The area of contact was mass produced urban culture: movies, advertising, science fiction, pop music. We felt none of the dislike of commercial culture standard among most intellectuals, but accepted it as a fact, discussed it in detail, and consumed it enthusiastically. One result of our discussions was to take Pop culture out of the realm of "escapism", "sheer entertainment", "relaxation", and to treat it with the seriousness of art. (quoted in Storey 2001: 149)

The new sensibility also questioned modernism's cultural elitism. Although modernism had often quoted from popular culture, most of the canon of modernist art had been deeply suspicious of most things popular. There could be little doubt that modernism's entry into the museum and the academy had been facilitated (despite its declared antagonism to "bourgeois philistinism") by its appeal to, and its homologous relationship with, the elitism of class society. Instead of causing outrage from the critical margins of bourgeois society, modernism had not only lost its ability to shock and disturb; it had become centered and canonized as the high culture of the modern capitalist world. Its subversive power had been drained by the academy and the museum. In a phrase, modernist culture has become official culture.

The new sensibility, therefore, was born in part out of a generational refusal of the categorical certainties of high modernism. In particular, modernism's insistence (now articulated from the center of official culture) on an absolute distinction between high and popular culture had come to be regarded as the "un-hip" assumption of an older generation. This was the first moment of postmodernism. As Andreas Huyssen (1986) observes, "Pop in the broadest sense was the context in which a notion of the postmodern first took shape, and from the beginning until today, the most significant trends within postmodernism have challenged modernism's relentless hostility to mass culture" (188).

Weird Scenes Inside the Goldmine: The Postmodern Condition

In the 1970s, the new sensibility became the postmodern condition. What had been, at least in part, a celebration of the mixing of high and low was now a reason for despair or grumbling resignation. It was two French theorists, Jean-François Lyotard (1984) and Jean Baudrillard (1983), who did most to change the cultural map. However, rather than discuss their work, I want to look instead, because

64

of its specific focus on popular culture, at the postmodern condition as described (under the influence of Lyotard and Baudrillard) by the American Marxist cultural critic, Fredric Jameson.

According to Jameson, postmodernism is "the cultural dominant . . . of late capitalism" (1984: 85). This represents "the purest form of capital yet to have emerged, a prodigious expansion of capital into hitherto uncommodified areas." Unlike modernism, which taunted the commercial and the commodified, postmodern culture, rather than resisting, "replicates and reproduces . . . the logic of consumer capitalism" (1983: 125); "it reinforces and intensifies it" (1984: 85). As a result, "aesthetic production . . . has become integrated into commodity production generally" (56). Culture is no longer ideological, disguising the economic activities of capitalist society; it is itself an economic activity, perhaps the most important economic activity of all.

Jameson claims that postmodernism is a "schizophrenic" culture. He uses the term in the sense developed by Jacques Lacan (1977) to signify a language disorder, a failure of the temporal relationship between signifiers. The schizophrenic experiences time not as a continuum (past–present–future), but as a perpetual present, which is only occasionally marked by the intrusion of the past or the possibility of a future. The "reward" for the loss of conventional selfhood (the sense of self as always located within a temporal continuum) is an intensified sense of the present – what Dick Hebdige (1998) calls "acid perspectivism" (suggesting that the experience Jameson describes is similar to "tripping" – being under the influence of the the hallucinogenic drug LSD). To call postmodern culture "schizophrenic" is to claim that it has lost its sense of history (and its sense of a future different from the present). It is a culture suffering from "historical amnesia," locked into the discontinuous flow of a perpetual present. The temporal culture of modernism has given way to the spatial culture of postmodernism.

Although postmodernism is a culture without a sense of history, it is nevertheless a culture which feeds vampirically on the past. Jameson argues that postmodernism is a world of pastiche: a world

65

in which stylistic invention and innovation is no longer possible. Given this, "the producers of [postmodern] culture have nowhere to turn but to the past: the imitation of dead styles, speech through all the masks and voices stored up in the imaginary museum of a now global culture" (65). Instead of original cultural production, there is said to be only cultural production born out of previous cultural production. In short, according to Jameson, it is a culture which "involve[s] the necessary failure of art and the aesthetic, the failure of the new, the imprisonment in the past" (1983: 116). It is therefore a culture "of flatness or depthlessness, a new kind of superficiality in the most literal sense" (1984: 60). A culture of images and surfaces, without "latent" possibilities, it derives its hermeneutic force from other images, other surfaces, the interplay of intertextuality – what Jameson refers to as the "complacent play of historical allusion" (1988: 105). Therefore, rather than a culture of pristine creativity, postmodern culture is said to be a culture of quotations.

Jameson's best-known example of the practice of pastiche in postmodern culture is what he calls the "nostalgia film." The category could include a number of films from the 1980s and 1990s: *Back to the Future I, II*, and *III* (1985, 1989, 1990), *Peggy Sue Got Married* (1986), *Rumble Fish* (1983), *Angel Heart* (1987), *Blue Velvet* (1986). As he insists, the nostalgia film is not just another name for the historical film. This is clearly demonstrated by the fact that his own list includes the *Star Wars* trilogy. Now it might seem strange to suggest that a film about the future can be nostalgic for the past, but as Jameson explains, "[*Star Wars*] is metonymically a . . . nostalgia film . . . it does not reinvent a picture of the past in its lived totality; rather, [it reinvents] the feel and shape of [a] characteristic art object of an older period" (1983: 116). Therefore, according to Jameson, the nostalgia film works in one or two ways: it recaptures and represents the atmosphere and stylistic features of the past, and it recaptures and represents certain styles of viewing of the past. What is of crucial significance for Jameson is that such films do not attempt to recapture or represent the "real" past, but always make do instead with certain cultural myths and stereotypes about the past. They offer what he calls "false realism," films about other films, representations of other representations. History is effaced by "historicism . . . the random cannibalisation of all the styles of the past, the play of random stylistic allusion" (1984: 65–6). He insists that our awareness of the play of stylistic allusion

> is now a constitutive and essential part of a film's structure: we are now in "intertextuality" as a deliberate, built-in feature of the aesthetic effect, and as the operator of a new connotation of "pastness" and pseudo-historical depth, in which the history of aesthetic styles displaces "real" history. (67)

Austin Powers: The Spy Who Shagged Me (1999) could be cited as a very profitable example of the random cannibalization of the past. The movie is said to have grossed almost 55 million dollars within a week of its release in the USA (Floyd 1999: 77), increasing to 100 million dollars in two weeks (Palmer 1999: 78). As Mike Myers (the film's writer, producer, and principal star) himself explains, "I'm a police composite of every comedian I've ever liked, Peter Sellers, Alec Guinness, Dan Aykroyd, John Belushi, Woody Allen, *Monty Python*, *The Goodies*, the British TV show *Some Mothers Do 'Ave 'Em*, *On the Buses*, the *Carry On* films" (quoted in Floyd 1999: 78). Moreover, Myers' account of the origins of Austin Powers could also be cited as evidence of Jameson's argument about the random cannibalization of the past, "Austin Powers is everything I watched [on TV in the late sixties]" (quoted in Duncan 1999: 18). Indeed, the very character of Austin Powers can himself be seen as symptomatic of the process Jameson describes; he was cryogenically frozen in 1967 and unfrozen in 1997. Even this plot could be seen as a Jamesonesque "quotation" from the past – Myers' story-line almost certainly being indebted to the BBC action series *Adam Adamant* (1966–7), in which an Edwardian adventurer entombed in a block of ice since 1902 is defrosted amid the coffee bars and fashion boutiques of 1960s "Swinging London."

I think there are two responses that can be made to Jameson's position. The first is to point to the fact that most of the despair and "cultural pessimism" generated by the supposed postmodern condition is an attitude and a perspective which has run concomitant with the development, since the nineteenth century, of what is usually described pejoratively as mass culture. If we situate Jameson's critique of postmodernism in this tradition, it can easily be shown to repeat points that we encountered in chapter 2 in the work of Arnold, the Leavisites, Eliot, Ortega y Gasset, Macdonald, but above all, in the work of the Frankfurt School. In a classic piece of Frankfurt School rhetoric, Jameson compares "the Utopian 'high seriousness' of the great modernisms" with postmodern culture's "essential triviality" (1984: 85). Moreover, he claims,

> the erosion of the older distinction between high culture and so-called mass or popular culture . . . is perhaps the most distressing development of all from an academic standpoint, which has traditionally had a vested interest in preserving a realm of high or elite culture against the surrounding environment of philistinism, of schlock and kitsch. (1983: 112)

Similarly, he writes of "the older kinds of folk and genuinely 'popular' culture which . . . from the mid-nineteenth century on, have gradually been colonised and extinguished by commodification and the market system" (1988: 112).

The supposed extinction of a genuine culture of the people, together with the claim that high culture has been sucked into the degraded domain of commodified mass culture, produces again what sounds remarkably like the standard Frankfurt School/Leavisite dismissal of popular culture. Lawrence Grossberg (1988: 174) describes Jameson's position with economy:

> For Jameson . . . [t]he masses . . . remain mute and passive, cultural dopes who are deceived by the dominant ideologies. . . . Hopeless they are and shall remain, presumably until someone

else provides them with the necessary maps of intelligibility and critical models of resistance.

As we discussed earlier, the response of the postmodern "new sensibility" to modernism's canonization was a re-evaluation of popular culture. The postmodernism of the 1960s was therefore in part a "democratic" attack on the elitism of modernism. It signaled a refusal of what Andreas Huyssen (1986: viii) calls "the great divide . . . [a] discourse which insists on the categorical distinction between high art and mass culture." According to Huyssen, "To a large extent, it is by the distance we have travelled from this 'great divide' between mass culture and modernism that we can measure our own cultural postmodernity" (57). It is clearly the case that Jameson has not himself traveled very far beyond the great divide. Mike Featherstone (1991: 9) detects a certain nostalgia in Jameson's position: "he is nostalgically bemoaning the loss of authority of the intellectual aristocracy over the population." In similar fashion, John Docker (1994: 128) poses the question, "Is Fredric Jameson the F. R. Leavis of the postmodern world? Is 'Postmodernism, or the Cultural Logic of Late Capitalism' [Jameson 1984] yet another rewriting, in the modernist palimpsest, of 'Mass Civilisation and Minority Culture'?" Bryan Turner's (1987: 153) general point about intellectuals and popular culture may have particular relevance to Jameson's position.

> Intellectuals find it difficult to come to terms with the egalitarian implications of mass consumption, since intellectual culture is based upon the assumption that knowledge can only be achieved through the asceticism of disciplined education. Mass education, mass culture, modern systems of transport and contemporary forms of consumerism are generally criticised as a falsification of genuine standards, individual freedom and the autonomy of educated tastes.

The second response that can be made to Jameson's position is to point to the fact that what is being claimed as new is really only an acceleration and intensification of what has been happening in the traditions of popular entertainment since at least the nineteenth century. In other words, what Jameson (and others like him) identify as postmodern culture has always been a feature of *modern* popular culture. As David Chaney (1994: 204) observes,

> the privileged qualities of postmodernism – parody/pastiche, depthlessness, allegory, spectacular show, and an ironic celebration of artifice – have all been central to the submerged traditions of popular culture. One has only to think of the traditions of music hall and vaudeville, the fair-ground, the circus and pantomime, the melodramatic theatre and the literatures of crime and romance to find all these qualities clearly displayed.

Elizabeth Wilson (1998: 399) makes a similar point with regard to fashion: "some of the themes and hallmarks of what is today termed postmodernism have been around for a long, long time." She maintains that "Fashion [which she describes 'as the most popular aesthetic practice of all' (400)] . . . has relied on pastiche and the recycling of styles throughout the industrial period" (393). There may, therefore, be a certain (postmodern) irony in Jameson's complaint about nostalgia effacing history, given that his own critique is structured by a profound nostalgia for modernist "certainty," promoted, as it is, at the expense of detailed historical understanding of the traditions of popular entertainment.

Postmodern Hyperconsciousness

Jim Collins (1993: 248) has identified what he calls an "emergent type of genericity": popular films which "quote" other films, self-consciously making reference to and borrowing from different genres of film. What makes Collins' position more convincing than Jameson's is his insistence that such films appeal to (and help constitute) an audience of knowing bricoleurs, who take pleasure from

70

this and other forms of bricolage. Whereas Jameson argues that such forms of cinema are characterized by a failure to be truly historical, Peter Brooker and Will Brooker (1997: 7), following Collins, see instead "a new historical sense . . . the shared pleasure of intertextual recognition, the critical effect of play with narrative conventions, character and cultural stereotypes, and the power rather than passivity of nostalgia."

Brooker and Brooker argue that Quentin Tarantino's films

> can be seen as reactivating jaded conventions and audience alike, enabling a more active nostalgia and intertextual exploration than a term such as "pastiche", which has nowhere to go but deeper into the recycling factory, implies. Instead of "pastiche", we might think of "re-writing" or "re-viewing" and, in terms of the spectator's experience, of the "re-activation" and "re-configuration" of a given generational "structure of feeling" within a more dynamic and varied set of histories.

Andrew Goodwin (1991: 175) makes similar claims for the use of "sampling" in pop music. He argues that sampling is often "used to invoke history and authenticity" and that "it has often been overlooked that the 'quoting' of sounds and styles acts to historicize contemporary culture." Pastiche just does not adequately describe the ways in which "contemporary pop opposes, celebrates and promotes the texts it steals from" (173). In the main, pop music still tends to operate with an aesthetic which drifts between Romanticism's tortured genius and modernism's avant-garde artist. Because of this, sampling is rarely, if ever, done as a form of pastiche (or even parody); samples are incorporated into the "organic whole" in much the same way as in T. S. Eliot's classic monument to modernist poetic practice, *The Waste Land* (1922).

According to Collins (1993: 246), part of what is postmodern about western societies is the fact that the old is not simply replaced by the new, but is recycled for circulation together with the new. As he explains, "The ever-expanding number of texts and technologies is both a reflection of and a significant contribution to the 'array' – the perpetual circulation and recirculation of signs that forms the fabric of postmodern cultural life." He argues that "This foregrounded, hyperconscious intertextuality reflects changes in terms of audience competence and narrative technique, as well as a fundamental shift in what constitutes both entertainment and cultural literacy in [postmodern culture]" (250). As a consequence of this, Collins argues (with specific reference to cinema) that "Narrative action now operates at two levels simultaneously – in reference to character adventure and in reference to a text's adventures in the array of contemporary cultural production" (254). The widespread eclecticism of postmodern culture is encouraging and helping to produce what Collins calls the "sophisticated bricoleur" of postmodern culture (337). For example, television programs such as *Twin Peaks* and *The Simpsons* both constitute audiences as bricoleurs and in turn are watched by audiences who celebrate their bricolage. In this way, then, "Not only has reception become another form of meaning production, but production has increasingly become a form of reception as it rearticulates antecedent and competing forms of representation" (338).

Postmodern culture is saturated by media. This is most visible in the way television (in a effort to fill the space opened up by the growth in satellite and cable channels) recycles its own accumulated past, and that of cinema, and broadcasts these alongside what is new in both media. But this does not mean that we must despair in the face of Jameson's postmodern imposed "structure"; rather we should think in terms of both "agency" and "structure" – which ultimately is always a question of "articulation" (Hall 1996a, Storey 1999). Collins (1992: 334) provides this example of different strategies of articulation:

The Christian Broadcasting Network and Nickelodeon both broadcast series from the late fifties and early sixties, but whereas the former presents these series as a model for family entertainment the way it used to be, the latter offers them as fun for the contemporary family, "camped up" with parodic voice-overs, super-graphics, reediting designed to deride their quaint vision of American family life, which we all know never really existed even "back then."

There can be little doubt that similar things are happening in, for example, advertising, cinema, fashion, music, and in the different lived cultures of everyday life. It may not be a sign that there has been a general collapse of the distinctions people make between, say, high culture/popular culture, past/present, history/nostalgia, fiction/reality; but it may be a sign (first noticed in the sixties, and gradually more so ever since) that such distinctions are becoming increasingly less important, less obvious, less taken for granted. But this does not, of course, mean that such distinctions cannot be, and are not being, articulated and mobilized for particular strategies of social distinction. In another account of the origins of Austin Powers, Myers points to something more complex than pastiche – a certain kind of parody, not of the sixties but of a particular way of understanding the sixties. As he explains,

> The movie [*Austin Powers: The Spy Who Shagged Me*] isn't about the 60s. If anything it's about straight culture's view of the 60s . . . It's something I noticed with my dad. He had mutton chops and dyed hair and he put in a bar downstairs at our house. He was like, "Hey, I'm still a swinger." It's the whole world of straight culture going, "I'm with it. Like the kids, you know?" That's what the whole Austin Powers thing is about . . . Austin Powers is like a huge in-joke that I never thought anyone else would get. (quoted in Braund 1999: 92)

Postmodern culture offers the possibility of many different articulations, and as Mike Myers warns us, we should not take any of these at face value; we must always be alert to the what, why, and for whom something is being articulated, and how it can always be articulated differently in other contexts.

Back to the Future: Opera Postmodern?

In recent years there have been signs that opera's status as the pinnacle of high culture is changing, as opera becomes more and more a feature of everyday cultural life (see Storey 2002 and 2003). Opera, for example, is now widely used in advertising: *Madame Butterfly* sells tea and orange juice, *The Barber of Seville* sells pasta sauce, cars, and cordless shavers, *Rigoletto* sells pizza and pasta sauce, *Lakmé* sells tissues, rice, crackers, and computers. Opera is also increasingly used on film soundtracks: *Raging Bull* is accompanied by *Tristan and Isolde*, *Gallipoli* by *The Pearlfishers*, *Scarface* by *Ernani*, *Hannah and her Sisters* by *Madame Butterfly*, *The Burbs* by *Rigoletto*, *The Witches of Eastwick* by *Turandot*, *Driving Miss Daisy* by *Rusalka*, *Babe* by *Carmen*, *Donnie Brasco* by *Nabucco*, *G.I. Jane* by *Gianni Schicchi*, *Man on the Moon* by *Lucia di Lammermoor*. The new public visibility of opera also includes opera stars performing with pop stars; opera stars hosting television variety shows; opera stars performing at the opening of major sporting events; opera stars having hit records.

As we discussed in chapter 3, removing opera from the world of everyday entertainment and redefining it as art was not just an organizational accomplishment; it also involved the introduction of a particular way of seeing opera – the aesthetic mode of consumption. Although opera once again attracts a popular audience, it confronts this audience as art that can be entertaining. But for it to be entertaining, it is now necessary for the new audience to do its "opera homework." It should, therefore, come as no surprise that the re-emergence of the possibility of opera as popular culture has been accompanied (and no doubt promoted) by the many books which have been published in the 1990s offering to educate the reader to appreciate opera. For example, there are now beginners' guides, rough guides, teach-yourself guides, guides for dummies, and crash-course guides. The fact that these books exist at all says a great deal about the success of the project to remove opera from the world of everyday entertainment.

74

The music industry has not been slow to see the commercial potential in the growing popularity of opera. Opera performers are increasingly marketed in much the same way as pop stars. José Carreras, Placido Domingo, Lesley Garrett, Angela Gheorghiu, Barbara Hendricks, Kiri Te Kanawa, Luciano Pavarotti, Leontyne Price, Andrea Bocelli are obvious examples of the opera singer as "pop star." There are also currently available a number of CD collections explicitly aimed at the newcomer to opera. Again their titles are drawn from the marketing techniques of pop music. For example, "The Only Opera Album You'll Ever Need," "The Best Opera Album in the World . . . Ever!" "Opera Hits," "The Ultimate Opera Collection," "Simply the Best Night at the Opera," "Opera to Die For," "World Opera Favourites," "The A to Z of Opera," "The Opera Album 2002."

The re-emergence of opera as popular entertainment has certainly not gone unresisted. There are those, like Canadian tenor Jon Vickers, who claim that opera is

> being invaded by those techniques that are corrupting our society – big PR, the personality cult, techniques which create hysteria but do not elevate man. They degrade our art . . . We cannot compromise . . . We mustn't smear the line between art and entertainment . . . You cannot bring art to the masses . . . You never will. (quoted in Levine 1988: 255)

Vickers is not alone in thinking this way. When Pavarotti gave a free concert in London's Hyde Park (July 30, 1991) and attracted an audience (despite the heavy rain) in excess of 100,000, the obvious popularity of the event appeared to threaten the class exclusivity of opera as high culture. An editorial in the UK magazine *Opera* (October 1991) wondered out loud: "Is Pavarotti the greatest known ambassador for opera, bringing untold thousands to its heady delights, or is he just a slightly unconventional but decidedly cuddly pop star?" This uncertainty was not shared by a reader's letter published in the same issue of the magazine:

75

I had the misfortune to attend Pavarotti's concert in Hyde
Park . . . I moved to various spots searching for a place from
which he could be heard to best advantage. In every place the
majority reaction of the audience was the same – they talked,
joked and laughed and occasionally jumped up and down to
see if they could see Pavarotti on the stage, pausing only to
produce thunderous applause at the end of each aria. It became
clear from all this that a Pavarotti event has very little to do
with opera as such, but everything to do with Pavarotti as a
phenomenon. Through continuous hype, he has now become
so famous that it is imperative to see him when he appears,
much as one visits Madame Tussaud's on coming to London,
or goes to see the three handed man at the fairground . . .
The argument that Pavarotti is a man of the people bringing
opera to the masses is a load of tosh, since the masses at Hyde
Park showed little interest in listening. At the end he was
vociferously applauded. Clearly the audience loved him; whether
they like opera is something else again. (quoted in Evans
1999: 355)

Situating Pavarotti in the company of waxwork figures and unusual
fairground exhibits is to threaten to undo what was done so successfully in the late nineteenth and the early part of the twentieth
century – the institutionalization of opera as high culture (see chapter 3). The very thought that an audience might have talked, joked,
laughed, and occasionally jumped up and down at the performance
of one of the great tenors of all time would be enough to make the
elite of nineteenth-century Boston and elsewhere turn despairingly
in their graves.

Is opera now postmodern? Has it become once again what it was
for most of the nineteenth century, a cultural practice that is understood as both art and entertainment, an integral part of a shared
public culture? What I think is happening is *almost* like a return to
the cultural relations of nineteenth-century Europe and the US.
However, there is one crucial difference between then and now. In

the nineteenth century, despite the fact that opera could be consumed by different social groups in different contexts and as part of different cultural practices, there was nevertheless a very real sense in which those who consumed opera consumed in effect the same opera. Although most of what now counts as opera (and it is a much broader range of texts and practices than existed in the nineteenth century) is an integral part of a shared public culture, there is one key part which is still as socially exclusive as it was intended to be when opera was first institutionalized as high culture – opera in the opera house. Although it is certainly true that opera has become more and more embedded in the cultural life of the everyday, there has been little sign of growth in the audience for opera as it is experienced in the prestigious opera houses of the UK and the US.[1] Therefore, to describe opera as popular culture is to identify only part of what has been happening to it in recent years. I think to see the whole picture is to see that opera is now, as it was for most of the nineteenth century, available for consumption as both elite and popular culture. Perhaps this is enough to make it postmodern.

6

Popular Culture as the "Roots" and "Routes" of Cultural Identities

Consumption is a significant part of the circulation of shared and conflicting meanings we call culture. We communicate through what we consume. Consumption is perhaps the most visible way in which we stage and perform the drama of self-formation. In this sense, then, consumption is also a form of production. When we meet someone for the first time, in order to get to know the kind of person they are, we ask certain questions. An obvious question to ask is what kind of work they do. But sooner or later, in order to get to know them better, we will ask questions about matters of consumption: what books do they read? what films do they watch? do they have favorite television programs? what kinds of music do they listen to? These, and many more like them, are all questions which connect consumption with questions of cultural identity. On knowing the answers to enough of these questions, we feel able to construct a cultural and social pattern and thus to begin to locate the person in a particular cultural and social space – we begin, in other words, to think we know who they are and what they are like.

In this chapter I will examine the relations between popular culture, practices of consumption, and identity formation. In particular, I will explore the roots and routes of cultural identities, that is, how our identities are formed between memory and desire; between memory, with which we seek to ground ourselves in a known past, and desire, which propels us through the present into an unknown future. But first, here are some general points about postmodern identities.

Postmodern Identities

Traditionally, identity has been understood as something coherent and fixed, an essential quality of a person that is guaranteed by nature, especially human biology ("human nature"). Over the course of the nineteenth century and the early part of the twentieth a number of major intellectual challenges were made to this way of seeing identity, each in its different way making a successful challenge to the idea of a fixed and coherent self. In different ways, Charles Darwin's theory of evolution (the evolving self), Karl Marx's concept of history (the situated self), Sigmund Freud's theory of psychoanalysis (the unconscious self), and Ferdinand de Saussure's theory of language (the self enabled and constrained in and through language), all helped to "decenter" the traditional concept of the fixed and stable self. Out of these challenges, and more recently out of the theoretical work of post-structuralism and postmodernism, another way to understand identity has emerged. This view posits identity, not as something fixed and coherent, but as something constructed and always in a process of becoming, but never complete – as much about the future as the past (Hall 1996b, 1996e). Most significantly of all, it is a concept of identity as constituted in history and culture and not something inherited from nature. It is also a formulation in which the concept of identity itself is replaced by the concept of identities, that is, multiple and mobile identities. Identities are, therefore, a form of "production" rather than the "consumption" of a fixed inheritance.

According to Stuart Hall (1996e: 4), "identities are about questions of using the resources of history, language and culture in the

79

process of becoming rather than being." Although identities are clearly about "who we think we are" and "where we think we came from," they are also about "where we are going." Identities are always a narrative of the self *becoming*. If you ask who I am, I will tell you a story. In this sense, as Hall points out, identities are increasingly less about "roots" and more about "routes." So, for example, I may be in one moment a supporter of Manchester United, at another a university professor, at another a father, and in another a friend. Each of these moments has an appropriate mode and context of articulation; that is, depending on context, our identities form particular hierarchies of the self. In particular contexts, the identity "in dominance" may be one thing, in another context it might be something quite different. But what will be the case is that these other nondominant identities are always present, always waiting, ready to play a part in the changing formation of the self. Therefore, in a situation where being a Manchester United supporter is my most important identity, how I might perform this identity may well be constrained by the fact that I am still a university professor.

Although we may all be the inventors of our selves, identities are made in conditions and circumstances which are rarely of our own making. Therefore, although identities are a sign of agency, identities are always made within structures and discourses, which both enable and constrain the making of identities. Moreover, identity formation is not something we can do alone. Our identities usually consist of a "negotiation" between the accumulation of autobiographical material (the narrative of the self) and the imposition of biographical material (the narrative of the self by significant others, including official records, such as medical, employment, criminal, academic ones). In this way, then, who we are is always a compromise between how we see ourselves and how we are seen by significant others. Identities are, therefore, a mixture of "interpellation" and "representation." On the one hand, cultural practices attempt to "interpellate" (Althusser 1998) or hale us into place as subjects of particular discourses; and on the other, modes of representation seek to construct us as particular subjectivities. In the first we are invited to occupy a subject position from which to "speak," while in the second we are located as subjects of which to be "spoken." To give a banal example: if I am stopped in the street by a pollster and I am asked if I like swimming and I answer yes, I have been interpellated into the subject position of someone who likes swimming. I can speak from this "subject position" as someone who likes swimming. Once I have gone my questioner can "represent" me as someone who likes swimming; I can be spoken of as someone who likes swimming. In this way, then, "Identities are . . . the points of temporary attachment to the subject positions which discursive practices construct for us" (Hall 1996e: 6).[1]

The Roots of Cultural Identities

A large part of who we are seems to belong in the past, that is, our sense of self seems grounded in our "roots." Our autobiographical narratives are primarily sustained by memory. Memory seems to be at the very core of identity; it connects who we are to who we once were. To explore the roots of cultural identities I will build my analysis on the concept of "collective memory," as developed in the work of French sociologist Maurice Halbwachs (1980). In order to be as clear as possible, I have divided Halbwachs' account of "collective memory" into four overlapping claims.

First, memory is as much collective as individual. Halbwachs explains this in two ways. First of all, like Freud, Halbwachs recognized that memories are often fragmented and incomplete. But whereas Freud searched for completion in the unconscious, Halbwachs argued that completion should be sought in the social world outside the individual. In other words, what is provisional in our own memories is confirmed by the memories of others. As he explains, "We appeal to witnesses to corroborate or invalidate as well as supplement what we somehow know already about an event . . . Our confidence in the accuracy of our . . . [memory]

increases . . . if it can be supported by others' remembrances" (22). This is not to deny that individuals have memories, which are their own, but to point to the ways in which individual and collective memories are promiscuously entangled and intermingled. That is, "the individual memory, in order to corroborate and make precise and even to cover the gaps in its remembrances, relies upon, relocates itself within, momentarily merges with, the collective memory" (50–1).

Think of what happens when a photograph album is produced at a family gathering. As the photographs are passed around, particular photographs cue memories for one family member, which are then supported, elaborated, or challenged by other members of the family. The discussions which ensue seek collectively to fix specific memories to particular photographs. In this way, family histories (and individual histories within the family) are rehearsed, elaborated, and (temporarily) "fixed."

Memory is also collective in another way. We sometimes remember what we did not ourselves experience firsthand. Halbwachs explains it like this,

> During my life, my national society has been a theater for a number of events that I say I "remember," events that I know about only from newspapers or the testimony of those directly involved . . . In recalling them, I must rely entirely upon the memory of others, a memory that comes, not as corroborator or completer of my own, but as the very source of what I wish to repeat. (51)

Child psychologist Jean Piaget gives this account of a powerful memory of a traumatic event he later learned he did not in fact experience:

> I was sitting in my pram, which my nurse was pushing in the Champs Elysées, when a man tried to kidnap me. I was held in by the strap fastened around me while my nurse bravely tried

to stand between me and the thief. She received various scratches . . . Then a crowd gathered, a policeman with a short cloak and a white baton came up, and the man took to his heels. (quoted in Loftus 1996: 62)

Piaget believed in this memory for more than a decade. When he was 15 years old, his parents received a letter from his former nurse, who was now a member of the Salvation Army. As he explains,

She wanted to confess her past faults, and in particular to return the watch she had been given as a reward on this occasion. She had made up the whole story, faking the scratches. I, therefore, must have heard, as a child, the account of this story, which my parents believed, and projected into the past in the form of a visual memory. (quoted in Loftus 1996: 62–3)

Halbwachs' second claim is that remembering is always a practice of reconstruction and representation. When we remember we do not resurrect a "pure" past. Memories are not veridical reports of past events. Memories may owe as much to rehearsal (both individual and collective) as they do to the particular details of actual past events. In this sense, remembering is a "production" and not a form of "consumption." This is not to deny the materiality of the past ("it actually happened"), but it is to insist that the past is mute, it has to be made to speak. Moreover, like culture generally, the past is "multi-accentual" (Volosinov 1973). That is, it can be made to speak in many different voices; it can be used to tell many different stories. For example, while it may be a fact that I did such and such a thing in the past, the meaning of what I did is not fixed in the past: it is always articulated, rehearsed, and elaborated in the context of the present. In other words, what signifies is not the "facts" but how the "facts" are interpreted, how they are articulated to make meaning in the present. Therefore, the profound interaction between memory and identity formation does not necessarily depend on the truth of what is remembered.

In a study of eyewitness testimony, Elisabeth Loftus (1996) shows how a person's memory for an event they had witnessed can be influenced and altered by exposure to additional information during the period between witnessing an event and recounting the event. The "post-event information" can have the effect of modifying, changing, or even supplementing the original memory. This results from a process social psychologists call "destructive updating" (Cohen 1996), in which what was originally remembered is displaced, trans- formed, and sometimes completely lost. What is true of eyewitness testimony is also true of memory in everyday life. What we remem- ber does not not stay the same; memories are forgotten, revised, reorganized, updated as they undergo rehearsal, interpretation, and retelling. The more important the event remembered, the more it is vulnerable to reconstruction, as it will be more frequently rehearsed, interpreted, and retold.

Halbwachs' third point is to argue that remembering is always situated in the present; memories do not take us into "the past," rather they bring "the past" into the present; remembering involves what psychologist Frederic Bartlett (1967: 227) calls an "effort after meaning." Remembering is in part about organizing and man- aging the past in relation to the present. The past is not pre- served and recalled, it is actively and continually constructed in the context of the present. In other words, remembering is about making meaning in the present and in response to the present. That is, in order for our memories to remain meaningful to us, they have to make sense in the context of the present. Interpretation will always be interpretation as informed by current attitudes and beliefs and not from the perspective of the context of the original memory. As Bartlett explains, memories "live with our interests and with them they change" (212). Put simply, our memories change as we change. As Halbwachs (1980: 69) himself explains, "a re- membrance is in very large measure a reconstruction of the past achieved with data borrowed from the present." To study memory, therefore, is not to study the past, but the past as it exists in the present. Thinking of, say, "national memory," it is the play of the

84

past in the present which makes memory and appeals to memory always potentially political – the power to use the past *to order* the present.[2]

Halbwachs' final point is that collective memory is embodied in mnemonic artifacts, forms of commemoration such as shrines, statues, war memorials, etc., what French historian Pierre Nora (1989: 7) calls "sites of memory."[3] Nora's "sites of memory" are much broader than Halbwachs' mnemonic artifacts. They include almost anything where memory can become anchored, for example, classroom textbooks, observing a minute's silence, reunion events. I think we can also add what I will call the "memory industries," that part of the culture industries concerned with articulating the past. Heritage sites and museums are obvious examples, but we should also include the mass media and popular culture more generally. The memory industries produce representations ("cultural memorials") with which we are invited to think, feel, and recognize the past.

There can be little doubt that memory has become more and more something we can retrieve from external sources. Such developments have persuaded Nora that

> Modern memory is, above all, archival. It relies entirely on the materiality of the trace, the immediacy of the recording, the visibility of the image . . . The less memory is experienced from the inside the more it exists only through its exterior scaffolding and outward signs . . . It adds to life . . . a secondary memory, a prosthesis-memory. (13–14)

Alison Landsberg (1995: 176) uses the term "prosthetic memories" to describe the ways in which mass media (especially cinema) may enable people to experience as memories what they did not themselves live. She claims that "What individuals see might affect them so significantly that the images actually become part of their own personal archive of experience" (179). Survivors of traumatic experiences often claim that they have difficulty distinguishing their personal memories from those produced by the "memory industries." For example, Vietnam veteran Williams Adams makes this telling point:

> When *Platoon* was first released, a number of people asked me, "Was the war really like that?" I never found an answer . . . because what "really" happened is now so thoroughly mixed up in my mind with what has been said about what happened that the pure experience is no longer there. This is odd, even painful, in some ways. But it is also testimony to the way our memories work. The Vietnam War is no longer a definite event so much as it is a collective and mobile script in which we continue to scrawl, erase, rewrite our conflicting and changing view of ourselves. (quoted in Sturken 1997: 86)

If what Halbwachs claims about memory is true, it has profound ramifications for the production of identities. Put simply, the "roots" of our identities are both present and absent, existing both inside our heads and outside in culture.

The Routes of Cultural Identities

Our identities may seem grounded in the past, but they are also about becoming who we want to be or being who we think we should be in particular contexts. That is, our identities are also in our "routes." It is possible to construct a model for thinking critically about the cultural routes of identity, using the work of the French post-structuralist psychoanalyst Jacques Lacan (1977).

Lacan argues that as infants we first exist as an amorphous mix of body parts and sensations in a preverbal world in which all our needs are met as if by magic. This is a world in which there is no distinction between subject and object or self and other; the infant is continuous with what surrounds it. The infant is complete, an integral part of the "full" world of the mother's body. This is a world of plenitude, in which infant and mother seem in perfect union. It is a realm of experience Lacan calls the "imaginary."

Lacan argues that a child's sense of self first emerges during what he calls the "mirror stage." Looking in a mirror (real or imagined), the child begins to see itself as a separate being (i.e. separate from its mother). For Lacan this is a process (which continues throughout the child's lifetime) of *misrecognition* (not the self, but an image of the self). As the child grows older, it will continue to make such identifications; seeing itself in a range of different images, objects, discourses, people . . . and by so doing the child will construct its sense of self (ego). Now knowing self and other, the "mirror stage" begins the child's journey into the realm Lacan calls the "symbolic."

Following successful transition through the Oedipus crisis,[4] the child enters the symbolic. This is the child's entry into language and culture. Language allows the child to communicate with others; thus it facilitates the distinction between subject and object (self and other). In this way language allows the child to articulate itself as "I." But language also draws attention to the fragility of our speaking self. For example, I am "I" when I speak to "you," and "you" when you speak to me. What seems inside is borrowed from outside. In this way, then, our sense of being a unique and complete individual is staged as something always slipping away. Therefore, although the child's subjectivity is made possible by language (without the symbolic realm of language the child would be unable to articulate its sense of self), it is also undermined by being articulated in language; language remains a structure forever outside the child's being, belonging to others in the same way as it belongs to it.

According to Lacan, then, our development is marked by a transition from the imaginary to the symbolic. It is a journey from the "nature" of the mother's body to the "culture" of language and selfhood. Once in the symbolic, the child is locked into the mechanisms of "desire." Desire is constituted and driven by "lack" – the impossibility of closing the gap (and the continual need to try) between the child's "self" and that which would make it whole again (the lost moment of plenitude when it existed in perfect union with the mother's body). The transition (although necessary) is so traumatic that we spend the rest of our lives trying to return; trying to get back to the fullness of the imaginary. This endless quest organizes the very narrative of our lives, a narrative in which we pursue substitute objects and engage in displacement strategies in a hopeless attempt to find the completion we had once known in the imaginary.

Perhaps the classic substitute object is romantic love. In the west we live in a world in which romantic love is held up as the ultimate solution to all our problems. Love is a narrative compelled by lack. If we find love it will make us whole again. The discourse of romance is the most fundamental displacement strategy. The promise that is made (and always broken) is a promise of a return to the blissful state of the imaginary. The "romance promise" can be found in many examples of popular culture. One very clear example is the song "Whole Again" by Atomic Kitten (2000), in which the line "You can make me whole again" is repeated nine times in the space of a three-minute song. Desire is here expressed as need. But desire is relentless and unsatisfiable; desire (driven by lack) is always what remains after needs and demands have been satisfied. The song seems to realize this: "My friends make me smile / If only for a while / You can make me whole again." Although the intention would seem to be to suggest that her friends can make her happy only for short periods, it also suggests that being made whole again can only ever be something temporary. Love stages and performs a dress rehearsal for an endlessly deferred moment of plenitude, the promise of a return journey that will never be made. Although love will not return us to the blissful condition of the imaginary, its emotional power makes it perhaps the most compelling substitute object.

What I hope I have suggested in terms of the roots and routes of identities is not just that our selves – our identities – are made *in* culture, rather than something we inherit from nature, but that even that which seems so personal, what we remember and what we desire, is itself inescapably entangled in culture. In other words, the roots and routes of identity are staged and performed in culture and with culture.

88

Mixing Memory and Desire: Dusty Springfield and "The Land of Love"

I said at the opening of this chapter that consumption is perhaps the most visible way in which we stage and perform the drama of self-formation, and moreover, that this should make us see consumption as a form of production. This is never more obvious than in the very active consumption practices of fans. To be a fan is to have a special relationship with objects of consumption. There is often an intense investment and a profound passion about consuming as a fan. But it is not just about buying records, reading articles, going to concerts, or wearing particular clothes; there is something more. Objects of fandom become a part of our sense of identity; they become embedded in the roots of memory and the routes of desire. Obsess us they may, but they can also empower. I know this from personal experience.[5]

It was as a troubled adolescent that I first started listening to Dusty Springfield. In a process of "cutting and pasting," I cannibalized the songs to make them bear secret significations. Phrases or single words were made to carry special meanings. I mentally rewrote the songs to fit the conditions of my listening. Determined to make them tell the stories I wanted to hear, I juggled the pronouns: "she" became "he," "he" became "she," "you" became "it," "I" became "you," "you" became "I," "it" became "you." Of course, the secret significations were not just made with words. I made meanings in the very texture of the music, in the "melodramatic" sounds, in the "melodramatic" musical settings. In "Anyone Who Had A Heart" (1964), for example, I listened repeatedly and with fascinated expectation for the sound of a ghostly figure breaking free from the chains that bound him. And then there was the power of her voice: the warm, colluding encouragement of her voice.

It was a combination of words, music, and voice which articulated for me a sense of what had happened in the past and what might happen in the future. Consuming the songs at the level of

89

connotation, valuing them for their "affective realism," enabled me to articulate my feelings (if only to myself and the "imaginary other" that was Dusty Springfield). Consumed in the way I consumed them, the songs offered a means of escape from a childhood I wished to forget and into a future I nervously longed to embrace, or at least part of my future – what Julia Kristeva (1989) calls "the land of love." The songs gave me a language in which to speak about the past and to anticipate a different future. The songs (consumed in the way I consumed them) put into words what I was feeling. What had been secret they made known; what had been hidden they made visible; what had been powerful in silence they made audible and weak. They made the past visible within the promise of a better future. In this way, the songs broadened my affective range of understanding and expression and increased my emotional capital.

I spent hours in a *fan*-tasy landscape I had created with and from these songs. It provided a curiously mirrored stage on which to try on and try out new and different identities. Mostly, the songs helped shift my sense of who I was and what I might become. I now know that my way of "reading" the songs was similar to the reading practice described by Michel de Certeau (1984: 174): a form of "textual poaching," in which "readers are travellers; they move across lands belonging to someone else, like nomads poaching their way across the fields they did not write." Similarly, I recognize my adolescent self in Henry Jenkins' (1992: 284) account of fan culture. Jenkins argues that fan reading is characterized by an intensity of intellectual and emotional involvement. As he insists,

> I am not claiming that there is anything particularly empowering about the texts fans embrace. I am, however, claiming that there is something empowering about what fans do with those texts in the process of assimilating them to the particulars of their lives. Fandom celebrates not exceptional texts but rather exceptional readings (though its interpretative practices make it impossible to maintain a clear or precise distinction between the two).

I think (in fact, I know) there was something empowering in what I did with the songs of Dusty Springfield. That's why they mattered to me.

Coda: Performing Identities

Our identities are not the expression of our "nature," they are a performance in culture. What Judith Butler (1999: 33) argues with regard to gender identities also, I think, applies to identities in general; that is, an "identity is performatively constituted by the very 'expressions' that are said to be its results." In this way, the performance of identity is the accumulation of what is outside (in culture) as if it were inside (in nature). In other words, our identities are made from a contradictory series of identifications, subject positions, and forms of representation which we have made, occupied, and been located in as we constitute and are constituted by performances that produce the narrative of our lives. Popular culture is a fundamental part of this process.

7

Popular Culture as Popular or Mass Art

Cultural Power

If aesthetics is, as I would argue, a way of seeing objects aesthetically, rather than a way of recognizing intrinsic aesthetic properties in objects, then there is no reason why we should not have an aesthetics of anything, including popular culture.[1] Moreover, if the aesthetic is not a property of things but a way of seeing things, there is no reason why the aesthetic gaze should generate a canon of texts. Therefore, I would argue, the production of canons, and cultural hierarchies more generally, are always the result of the play of cultural power. Barbara Herrnstein Smith (1988: 50–1) provides an excellent account of the process,

> What is commonly referred to as "the test of time" . . . is not, as the figure implies, an impersonal and impartial mechanism; for the cultural institutions through which it operates (schools, libraries, theaters, museums, publishing and printing houses, editorial boards, prize-awarding commissions, state censors, and so forth) are, of course, all managed by persons (who, by definition, are those with cultural power and commonly other forms of power as well); and since the texts that are selected

and preserved by "time" will always tend to be those which "fit" (and indeed, have often been designed to fit) their characteristic needs, interests, resources, and purposes, that testing mechanism has its own built-in partialities accumulated in and thus intensified by time.

Smith's point is that cultural hierarchies, rather than floating free of historical contingency, are continuously produced and reproduced by acts of implicit and explicit evaluation by people with the power to make their evaluations stick.

Raymond Williams (1998) makes a similar point when he refers to what he calls the "selective tradition." He argues that selection is always "governed by many kinds of special interests, including class interests." Therefore, rather than being a natural repository of what Arnold thought of as "the best that has been thought and said," it "will always tend to correspond to its *contemporary* system of interests and values, for *it* is not an absolute body of work but a continual selection and interpretation" (54). This suggests that the best way to think about matters of cultural value is to begin with power. Like value itself, the selective tradition is a construction; a construction, as Williams points out, which always articulates particular relations of cultural power. The selective tradition is always informed by particular class interests, speaking in specific social and historical contexts. In this way, what constitutes the selective tradition is as much about policing knowledge as it is about organizing terrains of critical inquiry. Therefore, although the making of a selective tradition may well be an inevitable outcome in encounters between academic discourse and cultural production, it is the attempt to deny agency and power (as if the "best" selected themselves) which must be articulated and resisted.

Cultural studies is not opposed to so-called high culture, but it is opposed to both the idea that this is a universal unchanging culture (simply "the best which has been thought and said"), and to the way in which high culture is mobilized to make, mark, and maintain social distinctions and class inequalities. Without the required cultural capital to decipher the "code" of the canonized object of art, people are made socially *vulnerable to* the condescension of those who have the required cultural capital. What is cultural is presented as natural, and, in turn, used to justify what is social. Like other ideological strategies, "The ideology of natural taste owes its plausibility and its efficacy to the fact that . . . it naturalises real differences, converting differences in the mode of acquisition of culture into differences of nature" (Bourdieu 1984: 68). Aesthetic relations thus mimic and help to reproduce social relations of power. As Bourdieu observes,

> the games of artists and aesthetes and their struggles for the monopoly of artistic legitimacy are less innocent than they seem. At stake in every struggle over art there is also the imposition of an art of living, that is, the transmutation of an arbitrary way of living into the legitimate way of life which casts every other way of living into arbitrariness. (57)

Bourdieu's work on cultural power is underpinned by his view of education. Rather than being a means to lessen inequality, education functions to legitimate it. He argues that the education system fulfills a quite specific social and political function, that is, to legitimate social inequalities which exist prior to its operations. It achieves this by transforming social differences into academic differences, and presenting these differences as if they were "grounded in nature" (387). The cultural tastes of dominant classes are given institutional form, and then, with deft ideological sleight of hand, their taste for this institutionalized culture (i.e. their own) is held up as evidence of their cultural, and ultimately their social, superiority. In this way, social distinction is generated by learned patterns of cultural consumption which are internalized as "natural" cultural preferences and interpreted and mobilized as evidence of "natural" cultural competencies, which are, ultimately, used to justify forms of class domination.

When Gravity Fails: An Aesthetics of Popular Culture?

In recent years there have been a number of attempts, especially by philosophers of aesthetics, to produce an aesthetics of popular culture. Noel Carroll (1998: 4), for example, starts from the premise that "mass art supplies a great many people with their aesthetic experience." To this end, he seeks to isolate "the common structural, functional, and ontological features of . . . mass art" (172).

Carroll rejects the view that the difference between high and popular culture is arbitrary, a convention articulated in the interest of those with social and economic power.[2] Instead he argues that what distinguishes mass art from art is first of all the way in which the former is produced, reproduced, and circulated by the mass media. This distinction would seem to be contradicted by the fact (which he concedes) that there are many examples of avant-garde art – not to mention high culture: Shakespeare, opera, ballet, etc. – which have also been produced, reproduced, and circulated by the mass media. In response to this objection, Carroll argues that it is really a question of intention: "clearly avant-garde artworks, when produced by means of mass media, are not mass artworks proper. For they are not designed for easy consumption by mass, indefinitely large, undifferentiated audiences" (189). The fact that mass art and avant-garde art can both use the same mode of dissemination would seem to suggest that the technology of mass media is not really a key factor in marking the difference between what are supposedly two quite distinct forms of art.

Carroll's second distinction is "ease of comprehension" (191). Here he concedes that Clement Greenberg was right when he claimed that mass art is "easy." He claims, however, that Greenberg misunderstood that "the ease with which mass art is consumed is not a flaw, but rather a design element, which is predicated on the function of mass art as an instrument for addressing mass audiences" (195). It is hard to see how knowing this would have made the

95

slightest bit of difference to Greenberg. Moreover, Greenberg (along with all the other "mass culture" theorists discussed in chapter 2) would have little difficulty accepting his next point:

> Mass artworks tend toward a certain kind of homogeneity exactly because they aim at engaging what is common among huge populations . . . [They are] intentionally designed to . . . [facilitate] accessibility with minimum effort, virtually on first contact, for the largest number of untutored (or relatively untutored) audiences. (196)

Carroll claims that in order to reach a "mass audience," mass art tends to gravitate toward

> certain types of content, like action/adventure stories . . . since it is easier for the average movie-goer to comprehend how a kick-boxer fights his way out of an ambush than it is to comprehend the intricate and crafty financial manoeuvrings of leveraged corporate take-overs or the behaviour of people with infinitely subtle sexual preferences. (205)

The idea that kick-boxing movies represent the very model of mass art does not seem to be borne out by the facts. *Titanic* is currently the highest-grossing film, with world receipts of 1.84 billion pounds (Ash 2001: 156). If we allow for inflation, *Gone With the Wind* would be top of the list, with box-office receipts of 2.37 billion pounds (*Guinness World Records*, 2001: 90). The other top ten highest-grossing films are *Star Wars: The Phantom Menace, Jurassic Park, Independence Day, Star Wars, The Lion King, E.T., Forrest Gump, The Sixth Sense, The Lost World: Jurassic Park*. There is little here to suggest that kick-boxing is the model for successful mass art. If we rank films in terms of attendance, thus avoiding the distortions of inflation, we get once again a list without a single kick-boxing film: *Gone With the Wind, Star Wars, The Sound of Music, E.T., The Ten Commandments,*

96

The Jungle Book, Titanic, Jaws, Doctor Zhivago, 101 Dalmatians (Ash 2001: 156).

Although Carroll (1998) wants to insist that "mass art" is art, he is all too willing to concede that it is very rarely as good as the real thing. Although he rejects the idea "that mass art is for its consumers an evolutionary waystation on a trajectory that culminates in modernism," he does insist that "the values available in mass art are on a continuum with the values of modernism" (48). Although he seems to want to resist the conclusion that the continuum between mass art and art is vertical, his approach seems to inexorably move him to that conclusion:

> Just as a taste for beer does not inevitably lead to a taste for champagne, an appreciation of the transactional value of mass art does not lead typical consumers to a taste for modernist art. And even persons attuned to the transactional values of modernist art can savour the perhaps often lesser virtues of mass art in the same way that a connoisseur of champagne can appreciate beer. Indeed, even the wine taster may think that beer is what one should have some of the time, even though she thinks that, overall, champagne is finer. And, of course, it is also true that thinking that overall champagne is superior to beer does not preclude the conviction that some beers can be superior to some champagnes. (48–9)

"Common sense" tells us that champagne is better than beer. But it does not tell us why. Moreover, I suspect that any attempt to explain why one is better than the other would very quickly become a discussion and an evaluation of the consumption practices of people. For such a discussion to be fully adequate it would have to take into account the historical movement of champagne's social status, including thinking about when it was available on draft in nineteenth-century music halls.

Carroll criticizes John Fiske (1989) for holding the view that popular culture is what people make in practices of consumption.

In particular, he dismisses Fiske's example of urban Aborigines in Australia who, when watching old Westerns on television, side with the Indians as they attack the wagon train or the homestead of white settlers. Carroll concedes that this is a possible response, but insists that "many of Fiske's urban aborigines [*sic*] must coincide perfectly with the responses the makers of the westerns in question intentionally designed their movies to elicit" (1998: 240). Leaving aside the difficulty of ever knowing whether a response coincides perfectly with an authorial intention, the idea of "convergence" rather than "difference" is present in Fiske's approach to popular culture. As I outlined in chapter 4, a concern with these different possibilities is a crucial aspect of cultural studies.

Fiske, and cultural studies more generally, would certainly disagree with Carroll's own sense of convergence and difference. Carroll claims that the urban Aborigines "could not have mobilised their differential, adversarial response, if they did not already, antecedently embrace the intended meaning of the sequences in question – namely, that these sequences represented white settlers being massacred" (241). This suggests that the meaning of a film is first of all so obvious that it is something we will all share; that is, our interpretations and the intentions of the makers will converge. Once this convergent meaning is "recognized" it is possible for a second meaning to be made, one that is different from the convergent meaning. Moreover, Carroll insists that the second level of meaning can only be made on the basis of having already recognized the first one.

What Carroll calls the first level of meaning, I think is better understood as a recognition of the "materiality" of a text, accessed through a description of its basic narrative – as the wagon train traveled west it was attacked by native Americans. It is around this kind of descriptive recognition that responses may converge and from which meanings can be made. Therefore, when Carroll says "these sequences represented white settlers being massacred," he is operating at the second level; he is interpreting the text on the basis of its recognized materiality. Now it may be true, and probably is true (otherwise why would Fiske bother paying attention to "oppositional" readings?) that most readings of the sequences in question have interpreted the events represented as a narrative of the massacre of white settlers by native Americans. But my point is this: such a reading is not simply dictated by the text itself. Alternative readings, informed by changing attitudes to American history, might refuse the idea that "massacre" is the only way to understand events. The text remains the same but how it is understood changes as the context of understanding changes. At the center of such contexts there is always a subject making meaning and thus making culture from and with a cultural object or a signifying practice.

Like Carroll, Richard Shusterman's (1992: 59) aim is to make the "case for widening art's borders to forms of popular culture." He seeks "not to abolish the institution of art but to transform it . . . [by] an opening of the concept of art to include popular arts whose support and satisfactions spread far beyond the socio-cultural elite" (140). Although I share his objective of bringing about a more democratic culture, I do not think this can be achieved by reforming the institution of art but only by ending the arbitrary and oppressive distinction between high and popular culture (which in this context always means low) as ready-made categories into which we can slot forms of cultural production. The problem with the distinction is that it weakens critical thought by predigesting evaluation: to fit the criteria of high or low does not require a judgment on quality or value. There is always a ready-made regime of evaluation in which something can be obviously art or obviously popular art or obviously mass culture regardless of any judgment that might be made about its cultural value. We instinctively know this when we concede that this is bad art and this is good popular art. As Shusterman points out, when people seek to justify the distinction they do so in terms of the best of high culture versus the most mediocre examples of popular culture,

Yet, unfortunately, there are many mediocre and even bad works of art, as even the most avid advocates of high culture

99

will admit. And just as high art is no unblemished collection of masterpieces, so . . . popular art is not an undifferentiated abyss of tastelessness where no aesthetic criteria are displayed or exercised. In both these types of art, the distinction between them being flexible and historical rather than rigid and intrinsic, there is room and need for aesthetic discrimination of success and failure. (172)

But if this is the case, it has profound ramifications in terms of the supposed difference between high and popular culture. Put simply, if bad art is possible, the category art must be an *a priori* form of classification, in which questions of intrinsic worth are always *post hoc* rationalizations. What Adorno and Horkheimer (1979: 137) claimed about the consumption of mass culture might be more appropriately applied to the consumption of high art: "No independent thinking must be expected from the audience; the product prescribes every reaction: not by its natural form (which collapses under reflection), but simply by signals." The signals which confront the consumer of high art are these: this is high art; you may decide that it is good or bad, but do not doubt that it is art; that has already been decided.

   For art to exist it requires the existence of "an autonomous field of artistic production . . . capable of imposing its own norms on both the production and consumption of its products" (Bourdieu 1984: 3). Therefore, to be art is not a matter of being culture of a particular quality, rather it is to conform to the changing demands of the institution of art. The institution of art is in part a machine for keeping in place the distinction between art and culture which is not art. The valorization of some culture which is not art as popular art can only reinforce the power of the institution of art to maintain the distinction which ultimately secures its existence. Introducing a few examples of popular culture may enlarge the realm of the aesthetic, but only at the cost of keeping in place a distinction on which arbitrary cultural exclusions continue to be made. What is required is not the selective expansion of the category of art, but an active undoing of the institutional work of the late nineteenth and early twentieth centuries, when middle-class elites first introduced the distinction. Why call it popular art? Why not simply say that it is art? To say popular art is to affirm the reality and status of art – the very institution that would insist on the qualifying term popular.[3]

Shusterman fully recognizes the relations of power articulated in the high/low divide. He believes, however, that popular art could "provide an alternative base . . . a promising force for transforming our concept and institutions of art" (145). He argues that "recognising their status as aesthetically legitimate cultural products would help reduce the socially oppressive identification of art and aesthetic taste with the socio-cultural elite of high art." But why would it? It would just perpetuate the cultural distinction between high and popular culture and the social distinction between those for whom culture is high or popular. Such reforms, as proposed by Shusterman, will only entrench these distinctions. Allowing that some popular culture is also art (albeit popular art) can only reinforce the arbitrary and socially oppressive distinction between high and popular culture. It seems like special pleading, in which the distinction is seen as valid, only that the line needs a little adjustment in order to admit, say, some examples of rock music. His argument is further weakened by his uncritical articulation of "the ideology of mass culture" (Storey 2001: 146):

> the ruling class . . . under the guise of democratic populism . . . exploits the arts of popular culture and the manipulative art of advertising to promote docile conformism and worship of the new which keeps the dominated consumer in a confused frenzy of changing fashion and consequent insecurity about his tastes. In contrast, high art (along with education) represents . . . the only serious rival to material capital and conspicuous consumption as a source of social status and legitimation, even if we regret that much of its legitimating potential comes from its traditional class markings.

101

It may even be a mistake to suppose that Shusterman thinks that popular art is "the best that has been thought and said" of popular culture: "I admit that the products of popular art are often aesthetically wretched and lamentably unappealing, just as I recognize that their social effects can be very noxious, particularly when they are consumed in a passive, all-accepting way" (176). It seems that in the end popular art is to be valued only for its "potential" (177).

Cultural studies has been here before. Almost four decades ago Stuart Hall and Paddy Whannel published *The Popular Arts* (1964). The argument of the book was that "in terms of actual quality . . . the struggle between what is good and worthwhile and what is shoddy and debased is not a struggle *against* the modern forms of communication, but a conflict *within* these media" (15). Hall and Whannel set themselves the task to develop "a critical method for handling . . . problems of value and evaluation" in the study of popular culture.

Like Carroll and Shusterman, they argue that within popular culture there is a distinct category they call "popular art." Popular art is not art which has attempted and failed to be "real" art, but art which operates within the confines of the popular. They offer this definition of popular art: "while retaining much in common with folk art, it . . . is no longer directly the product of the 'way of life' of an 'organic community', and is not 'made by the people', it is still, in a manner not applicable to the high arts, a popular art, for the people" (59).

Again like Carroll and Shusterman, rather than confront the ideology of mass culture, they seek instead to privilege and thus to remove certain of the texts and practices of popular culture from the condemnation of the critics of mass culture. Popular art, therefore, is mass culture which has risen above its origins. Unlike "average films or pop music [which] are processed mass art," popular art is, for example, the "best cinema," the "most advanced jazz" (78). They claim that, "Once the distinction between popular and mass art has been made, we find we have bypassed the cruder generalisations about 'mass culture', and are faced with the full range of material offered by the media."

102

The main focus of *The Popular Arts* is on the textual qualities of popular culture. However, when they turn to questions of youth culture they find it necessary to discuss the interaction between text and audience. They recognize that to do full justice to the relationship, they have to include other aspects of teenage life: "work, politics, the relation to the family, social and moral beliefs and so on" (269). They concede that the claim that "the picture of young people as innocents exploited" by the pop music industry "is over-simplified." Against this, they argue that there is very often conflict between the use made of a text by an audience and the use intended by the producers. Significantly, they observe, "This conflict is particularly marked in the field of teenage entertainments . . . [although] it is to some extent common to the whole area of mass entertainment in a commercial setting" (270). Pop music culture – songs, magazines, concerts, festivals, comics, interviews with pop stars, films, etc. – helps to establish a sense of identity among youth:

> The culture provided by the commercial entertainment market . . . plays a crucial role. It mirrors attitudes and sentiments which are already there, and at the same time provides an expressive field and a set of symbols through which these attitudes can be projected . . . Teenage culture is a contradictory mixture of the authentic and manufactured: it is an area of self-expression for the young and a lush grazing pasture for the commercial providers. (276)

Pop music exhibits "emotional realism"; young men and women "identify with these collective representations and . . . use them as guiding fictions. Such symbolic fictions are the folklore by means of which the teenager, in part, shapes and composes his mental picture of the world" (281). Hall and Whannel also identify the way in which teenagers use particular ways of talking, particular places to go, particular ways of dancing, and particular ways of dressing to establish distance from the world of adults: they describe dress style as "a minor popular art . . . used to express certain contemporary

103

attitudes . . . for example, a strong current of social nonconformity and rebelliousness" (282). This line of investigation would come to full fruition in the work of Birmingham University's Centre for Contemporary Cultural Studies, carried out during the 1970s, under the directorship of Hall himself (Storey 2001).

Beyond Aesthetic Essentialism

The fundamental problem with approaches which privilege the aesthetic, regardless of how "democratic" their intent, is that they always lead to cultural objects and practices being separated in terms of their textual properties. To think, therefore, in terms of aesthetic value is to think outside the material and historical concerns of cultural studies; inevitably it leads to an argument that sees cultural practices which are defined as art as existing in some magical way outside historical and social contingencies, that is, as transcending the social and the historical, whereas cultural practices which are defined as non-art are embedded in the historical and social and can be explained in terms of this embeddedness.

Although I recognize that evaluation is a core practice in the making of culture, I refuse to limit this to questions of purely aesthetic value, worrying over whether or not something is good or bad in some mythical and mystical universal sense, rather than say, good for this, bad for that, etc. To worry in that way is to engage in the aesthetics of the finishing school (culture as private self-improvement). I think that cultural studies should interrogate instead the strategies of value and evaluation, knowing that evaluation is never a "disinterested" practice. It is always entangled with other forms of judgment – political, ethical, commercial, etc.; it is always situated in arguments for or against something or someone. Therefore, when we argue that something is good or bad, we should always be clear about for whom it is good or bad or for what it is good or bad.

Like meaning, evaluation is a social production, a human practice. Just as the world has to be made to mean, things have to be evaluated,

given a value. Objects do not have a value which is inside waiting to be discovered: evaluation is what happens when an object
is consumed. Aesthetic approaches make a fetish of value: what
derives from practices of human perception is magically transmuted
to become a fixed property of an object. Against this, I would insist
that the value of something is produced in its use (the coming
together of subject and object); it is not in the thing itself. The
trouble with aesthetic approaches is that they drain the world of
both the activity and the agency which goes into the making of
evaluations; they inevitably reduce culture to a property of objects.
Inevitably, "textual fetishism" produces two things: an imaginary
museum of objects to be preserved, and a pedagogy which insists
that people have to be trained to recognize the intrinsic values of
selected objects, which invariably leads to a division being drawn
between the minority who can and the majority who cannot. In
this way, aesthetic value can be used as a mechanism to exclude.

Too often when aesthetics and popular culture are discussed together it is for the purpose of establishing evaluative boundaries
between "the best that has been thought and said" and the rest. This
sometimes involves the redefinition of some texts and practices,
previously considered as belonging to popular culture, now being
revalued to allow them to cross from the rest to the best. Once this
has been done, the difference between the two supposedly distinct
aesthetic categories, and the need to police the difference between
them, is once again confirmed. The aesthetics of the popular almost
inevitably leads to a "game" in which the distinction between high
and popular is reinforced and thus made more secure. As Bourdieu
(1984: 569) explains,

> The struggles which aim . . . to transform or overturn the legit-
> imate hierarchies through the legitimating of a still illegitimate
> art or genre . . . are precisely what creates legitimacy, by creat-
> ing belief not in the value of this or that stake but in the value
> of the game in which the value of all the stakes is produced
> and reproduced.

105

Instead of playing this game, we should evaluate the cultural field as a whole; and when we say popular culture (whether in terms of particular texts or modes of appropriation) we should seek only to distinguish it from nonpopular culture; in other words, to say popular culture should mean nothing more than an indication of quantity and not quality.

However, although the distinction between high and popular culture has no basis in the properties of texts and practices, this should not lead us to ignore the institutional embeddedness of this distinction. What should be examined, therefore, is not the distinction at the level of textuality but how the distinction is maintained and deployed in institutional strategies of power.

8

Popular Culture as Global Culture

Globalization

Globalization is the name given to the complex relations which characterize the world in the twenty-first century. It refers to the relentless global flow of capital, commodities, and communications across increasingly porous territorial boundaries. National borders are becoming less and less important as transnational corporations, existing everywhere and nowhere, do business in a world economy.

Globalization also describes what is called "time–space compression" (Harvey 1990: 240): the way in which the world appears to be shrinking under the impact of new electronic media, like satellite television and the internet, which facilitate the extending of social relations across time and space. Time and space no longer dictate the range of my relationships. Being near or being distant no longer organizes with whom I communicate. Electronic media (fax, telephone, e-mail, the internet) give me access to a world well beyond my "local" community. I may communicate more with people in Taiwan, Australia, Germany, the US, via e-mail, than I do with neighbors who live within 200 meters of my house. In this sense, the global may be more local than the local. Similarly, television news provides me with images and information about events that are taking place thousands of miles away from where I live. Unless

I watch the "local" news or read the "local" paper, it is likely that I will be better informed about "global" events than I am about "local" events.

Time–space compression brings into close contact images, meanings, ways of life, cultural practices, which would otherwise have remained separated by time and space. This can produce a certain homogeneity of cultural experience or resistance in defense of a previous way of life, or it can bring about a mixing of cultures, producing forms of "hybridization." Nor should hybridization be seen as another name for coping with cultural imperialism; western societies also absorb and adopt cultural practices from elsewhere.[1]

This aspect of globalization may be experienced by simply walking down the "local" high street, where "local" goods are displayed alongside "global" goods gathered in from around the world. We encounter the global in the clothes we wear, the music we listen to, the television programs and films we watch. Perhaps it is most visible in the food we eat. The culinary pluralism of, for example, most British towns and cities, where fish and chips compete with curries, kebabs, chilies, stir fries, pizzas and pasta, is clearly the sign of the globalization of the High Street menu. It is easy to object that we are not being given access to "authentic" cuisine, but authentic or not (and how much cuisine is really authentic?), it is understood as, for example, Indian, East African, Thai, Turkish, Mexican, Chinese, and Italian. It has certainly changed the cultural experience of eating out (and eating in via takeaways), so much so that chicken tikka masala is now regarded as the most popular *British* dish.

Globalization also refers to the increasing global mobility of people. It may force workers to travel thousands of miles in search of paid employment. Think of something as everyday as football. Over the last few years the English Premier League has featured professional players from around the world: Algeria, Argentina, Australia, Austria, Belgium, Bermuda, Bosnia, Brazil, Bulgaria, Cameroon, Canada, Chile, China, Colombia, Congo, Costa Rica, Croatia, Czech Republic, Denmark, Eire, Ecuador, Estonia, Finland, France, Germany, Greece, Holland, Iceland, Israel, Italy, Jamaica, Japan, Latvia,

Liberia, Morocco, Nigeria, Northern Ireland, Norway, Peru, Poland, Portugal, Russia, Scotland, South Africa, Spain, Sweden, Switzerland, Trinidad, Turkey, Ukraine, Uruguay, United States, Venezuela, Wales, and Yugoslavia. Professional footballers who travel the globe in search of paid employment are certainly the glamorous and wealthy end of labor migration but they are, nevertheless, a sign of a global economy.

Trading Commodities for Culture in the American Global Village

One dominant view of globalization is to see it as a process of homogenization, that is, as the reduction of the world to an American "global village" (McLuhan 1967), where everyone speaks English with an American accent, wears Levi jeans and Wrangler shirts, drinks Coca-Cola, eats at McDonalds, surfs the net on a computer overflowing with Microsoft software, listens to rock or country music, and watches a mixture of MTV, CNN news broadcasts, Hollywood movies, reruns of Dallas, and discusses the prophetically named World Series, while drinking a bottle of Budweiser or Miller and smoking Marlboro cigarettes. In this scenario globalization is the successful global imposition of Americanization, in which the economic success of US capitalism is underpinned by the ideological work that its commodities supposedly do in effectively destroying indigenous cultures and imposing an American way of life on "local" populations.

American sociologist Herbert Schiller (1979), for example, claims that the ability of American transnational companies to successfully unload commodities around the globe is producing an American global capitalist culture. The role of media corporations, he claims, is to make programs which "provide in their imagery and messagery, the beliefs and perspectives that create and reinforce their audiences' attachments to the way things are in the system overall" (30). In terms of the commodities which circulate as global culture there can be little doubt that the majority of these commodities originate from the US.[2] While this establishes a clear case for the economic power of the US, it does not prove that global culture is increasingly American culture.

There are fundamental problems with the argument that the cultural complexity of the world is being reduced to an American global village. For example, globalization as Americanization works with a very discredited account of the flow of influence: it simply assumes that it is possible to inject the dominant globalizing culture into a weaker local culture and in so doing replicate a version of the dominant culture. Now it is one thing to point to the successful ways in which capitalism as a global system has organized the world in terms of the commodity and the market, but it is quite another to then claim that the result is a homogenized world culture. It is only possible to think this if you already think that commodities equal culture in an obvious and straightforward way.

Globalization as Americanization is reductive in the particular sense that economic success is assumed to be the same as cultural imposition: the recognition of the obvious success of US multinationals at placing products in most of the markets of the world is understood as self-evidently ideological success. Success in the economic sphere equals success in the cultural sphere; in this way, the cultural is flattened into the economic, as if it were nothing more that a manifestation of an always reliable effect. Globalization as Americanization assumes that commodities are the same as culture; establish the presence of the former and you can predict the details of the latter. But as John Tomlinson (1999: 83) points out, "if we assume that the sheer global presence of these goods is *in itself* token of a convergence towards a capitalist monoculture, we are probably utilising a rather impoverished concept of culture – one that reduces culture to its material goods." It may be the case that certain commodities are used, made meaningful, and valued in ways which promote capitalism as a way of life, but this is not something which can be established by simply assuming that market penetration is the same as ideological penetration. Such a claim depends on an argument

110

which maintains that commodities have inherent values and meanings which are imposed on passive consumers. But if culture is the making and communication of meanings in contexts, then it is difficult to see how meanings made in one context can survive to be imposed in quite different contexts.

Another significant problem with globalization as Americanization, therefore, is that it operates with an extremely simplified notion of consumption. That is, it is assumed that audiences are the passive consumers of the cultural meanings which supposedly flow directly and unproblematically from the goods they consume. Hegemony is a complex and contradictory process: it is not the same as injecting people with "false consciousness." It is certainly not explained by the adoption of the assumption that "hegemony is prepackaged in Los Angeles, shipped out to the global village, and unwrapped in innocent minds" (Liebes and Katz 1993: xi). What are we to make of the global success of "hip hop"? Are South African, French, or British rappers the victims of American imperialism, the cultural dupes of a transnational music industry? This seems like a very difficult argument to sustain. A more interesting approach would be to look at how South African, French, or British youth have "appropriated" hip hop to meet their local needs and desires.

This is not to deny that capitalism is working – selling goods, making profits – but it is to deny that its success is the result of people being too stupid to realize that if they drink Coca-Cola or wear Levi jeans their indigenous culture will be destroyed and they will become Americanized.[3] A better way to understand the processes of globalization is one which takes seriously not just the power of global forces but also those of the local. This is not to deny power but to insist that a politics in which ordinary people are seen as mute and passive victims of a process they can never hope to understand, a politics which denies agency to the vast majority (or at best recognizes only certain activities as signs of agency) is a politics which can exist without causing too much trouble to the prevailing structures of global power.

111

Now it is certainly true that we can travel around the world while never being too far from signs of American commodities. What is not true, however, is that commodities equal culture. Globalization is not simply the production of a homogenized American global village in which the particular is washed away by the universal.[4] The process is much more contradictory and complex, involving the ebb and flow of both homogenizing and heterogenizing forces and the meeting and mingling of the "local" and "global" in new forms of hybrid cultures. Roland Robertson (1995) uses the term "glocalization" (a term borrowed from Japanese business) to describe globalization as the simultaneous interpenetration of the global and the local. In other words, what is exported always finds itself in the context of what already exists; that is, exports always become imports as they are incorporated into an indigenous culture.

To see globalization as Americanization is to repeat many of the ways of thinking we encountered in the discussion of popular culture as mass culture (see chapter 2). Principally, it is a mode of analysis which assumes that cultural commodities carry a monolithic message of manipulation, easily imposed on a passive audience, and thus winning them to the world view of the producers. Fortunately, consumption is not that straightforward: the global commodities of the culture industries always encounter people situated in local cultures. Consumption, therefore, is always an encounter between the materiality of a cultural commodity and the cultural formation of a consumer, which takes place in a particular context. Whether the outcome is manipulation or resistance, or a complicated mixture of the two, is a question which cannot be answered in advance of the actual encounter.

Globalization as Americanization also assumes that cultures can be lined up as distinct monolithic entities, hermetically sealed from one another until the fatal moment of the globalizing injection. Against such a view, Ien Ang (1996: 153) maintains that

the global and the local should not be conceived as two distinct, separate and opposing realities, but as complexly articulated, mutually constitutive. Global forces only display their effectivity in particular localities; local realities today can no longer be thought outside of the global sphere of influence, for better or for worse.

Similarly, Jan Nederveen Pieterse (1995: 45) argues that globalization is better understood "as a process of hybridization which gives rise to a global mélange." He points to "phenomena such as Thai boxing by Moroccan girls in Amsterdam, Asian rap in London, Irish bagels, Chinese tacos and Mardi Gras Indians in the United States, or Mexican schoolgirls dressed in Greek togas dancing in the style of Isadora Duncan" (53). To see globalization as simply a process of the export of sameness is to miss so much of what is going on.

It [globalization as homogenization] overlooks the countercurrents – the impact non-Western cultures have been making on the West. It downplays the ambivalence of the globalizing momentum and ignores the role of local reception of Western culture – for example, the indigenization of Western elements. It fails to see the influence non-Western cultures have been exercising on one another. It has no room for crossover culture – as in the development of "third cultures" such as world music. It overrates the homogeneity of Western culture and overlooks the fact that many of the standards exported by the West and its cultural industries themselves turn out to be of culturally mixed character if we examine their cultural lineages.

Globalization as Americanization also works with a very limited notion of the "foreign." What is foreign is presented as always a matter of national difference. But what is foreign can equally be a question of class, ethnicity, gender, sexuality, or any other marker of social difference. The foreign articulated at the level of the national may in fact hide divisions within the national itself. In other words, what is foreign at the level of the national may not be foreign at all at the level of, say, class or generation. In this way, then, what is foreign in terms of being imported from another country may be less foreign than differences already established by class or generation. Furthermore, the imported foreign may be used to "destabilize local hierarchies of taste and power" (Morley 1996: 331). Globalization can, therefore, both help confirm and help undo local cultures; it can keep one in place and it can make one suddenly feel out of place. For example, in 1946, addressing a conference of Spanish clerics, the Archbishop of Toledo wondered "How to tackle" what he called

> woman's growing demoralization – caused largely by American customs introduced by the cinematograph, making the young woman independent, breaking up the family, disabling and discrediting the future consort and mother with exotic practices that make her less womanly and destabilize the home. (quoted in Tomlinson 1997: 123)

Spanish women may have taken a different view.

Ang (1996) gives the example of the Cantonese Kung Fu movies which revitalized the declining Hong Kong film industry. The films are a mixture of "western" narratives and Cantonese values. As she explains,

> Culturally speaking, it is hard to distinguish here between the "foreign" and the "indigenous", the "imperialist" and the "authentic": what has emerged is a highly distinctive and eco- nomically viable hybrid cultural form in which the global and the local are inextricably intertwined, in turn leading to the modernized reinvigoration of a culture that continues to be labelled and widely experienced as "Cantonese". In other words, what counts as "local" and therefore "authentic" is not a fixed content, but subject to change and modification as a result of the domestication of imported cultural goods. (154–5)

Globalization is producing two contradictory effects, sameness and difference – that is, a sense that the world is becoming similar as it shrinks under the pressure of time–space compression, but also that it is characterized by an increasing awareness of difference. What on the surface may look like the export of sameness always involves the global being articulated with the local, and in the process having to compromise with local culture and tradition. Moreover, the processes of sameness may provoke the articulation of difference. Globalization is making the world smaller, generating new forms of cultural hybridity, but also bringing into collision and conflict different ways of making the world mean. While some people may celebrate the opening up of new global routes, other people may resist globalization in the name of local roots. Resistance in the form of a reassertion of the local against the insistent flow of the global can be seen in the increase in religious fundamentalism (examples can be found in Christianity, Hinduism, Islam, and Judaism) and the re-emergence of nationalism (most recently in the former Soviet Union and the former Yugoslavia).[5]

Rejecting the claim that globalization is really Americanization in disguise is not the same as saying that globalization is without power relations. The world is made up of many changing centers of power. Therefore, cultural flows can no longer be understood as moving from the American imperial center to the colonial periphery. Although this means that globalization may lack an obvious center, it is still marked by what Doreen Massey (1994: 149) calls "power geometry." Some people travel, some do not, and others travel because they are forced to move in search of work or away from political repression. Similarly, some people have the power to make things happen, while others seem to be always those to whom things happen, their lives continually shaped and structured by the powerful actions of unknown people from a distant elsewhere.

Massey makes the very perceptive point that many of the anxieties revealed in discussions of time–space compression may represent a particular political understanding of the world: a view from the West, unconsciously nostalgic for the simpler times of colonialism. As she explains, "The sense of dislocation which some feel at the sight of a once well-known local street now lined by a succession of

115

cultural imports – the pizzeria, the kebab house, the branch of the middle-eastern bank – must have been felt for centuries . . . by colonized peoples all over the world" (147) as they witnessed the importation of first British, then American institutions and commodities. She complains, quite rightly I think, about the fact that much of this writing is written "from the point of view of a (relative) elite. Those who today worry about a sense of disorientation and a loss of control must once have felt they knew exactly where they were, and that they *had* control" (165). Again, she detects "a predominantly white/First World" perspective on the question of the disruptive impact of the global on the local. This is particularly the case in the assumption that the penetration of the boundaries of the local is something of recent origin. To think this is to read history from the perspective of a colonizing First World:

> For the security of the boundaries of the place one called home must have dissolved long ago, and the coherence of one's local culture must long ago have been under threat, in those parts of the world where the majority of its population lives. In those parts of the world, it is centuries now since time and distance provided much protective insulation from the outside. (165–6)

The "Local" as the New Folk Culture

There is a great temptation to think of the local as authentic and the global as an inauthentic imposition. I think we should be careful to avoid romanticizing the local as the organic expression of a more "real" way of life. If we listen carefully it is possible to hear in the debates on the impact of the global on the local, echoes of earlier debates about folk culture being destroyed by industrialism and urbanism. It is as if the local is an authentic folk culture and the global is a homogenizing mass culture. But it is always more complicated than this: the global is always part of the local; the local is

116

what resists the global. As Edward Said (1993: xxix) observes, "all cultures are involved in one another; none is single and pure, all are hybrid, heterogeneous, extraordinarily differentiated, and unmonolithic."

> No one today is purely one thing. Labels like Indian, or woman, or Muslim, or American are now [no] more than starting points, which if followed into actual experience for only a moment are quickly left behind. Imperialism consolidated the mixture of cultures and identities on a global scale. But its worst and most paradoxical gift was to allow people to believe that they were only, mainly exclusively, White, or Black, or Western, or Oriental. (407–8)

Globalization offers the possibility of cultural mixing on a scale never before known. This can of course produce resistance to difference, but it can also produce the fusing of different cultures and the making of new and exciting forms of cultural hybridity.

Globalization is perhaps the final unwinding of the idea that for popular cultures to be truly authentic they have to be organically grounded in and bounded by a locality, the culture of Yorkshire or California. Globalized culture is clearly undermining what had been a key aspect in intellectual discussions of folk culture, that is, that being embedded in a particular space – the rural – and separated by both time and space from the development of modern urban and industrial life guaranteed "authenticity." The movement of people and commodities around the globe, bringing the global into the local, clearly challenges the idea that locality can fix the boundaries of a culture. The nomadic nature of global cultures suggests we are witnessing a shift in how we see cultures, a shift from culture as "roots" to culture as "routes."

To celebrate hybridity and forget about global power relations would be to miss even more than those who see globalization as homogenization. Cultural hybridity is not without its relations of power. As Nederveen Pieterse (1995: 57) observes, "hybridity raises

Table 8.1 Territorial cultures and translocal cultures
(from Nederveen Pieterse 1995: 61).

Territorial Cultures	*Translocal Cultures*
endogenous	exogenous
orthogenetic	heterogenetic
societies, nations, empires	diasporas, migrations
locales, regions	crossroads, borders, interstices
community-based	networks, brokers, strangers
organic, unitary	diffusion, heterogeneity
authenticity	translation
inward-looking	outward-looking
community linguistics	contact linguistics
race	half-caste, mixed-breed, métis
ethnicity	new ethnicity
identity	identification, new identity

the question of the *terms* of mixture, the conditions of mixing and mélange." He argues that the key factor in globalization as hybridity is that territorial cultures are being gradually overshadowed by translocal cultures (see table 8.1).

What I find particularly interesting about Nederveen Pieterse's categories is the way they can so easily be mapped on to the distinction we encountered in the first chapter of this book – that is, between folk culture and mass culture. But, again as he observes, "cultures have been hybrid *all along*, hybridization is in effect a tautology: contemporary accelerated globalization means the hybridization of hybrid cultures" (64). He argues that "Hybridity unsettles the introverted [territorial] concept of culture which underlies romantic nationalism, racism, ethnicism, religious revivalism, civilizational chauvinism, and culturalist essentialism." Moreover, "the very process of hybridization unsettles the introverted gaze, and accordingly, hybridization eventually ushers in post-hybridity, or transcultural cut and mix." The cultural landscape is changed utterly:

> In relation to the global human condition of inequality, the hybridization perspective releases reflection and engagement from the boundaries of nation, community, ethnicity, or class. Fixities have become fragments as the kaleidoscope of collective experience is in motion. It has been in motion all along and the fixities of nation, community, ethnicity and class have been grids superimposed upon experiences more complex and subtle than reflexivity and organization could accommodate.

Although it is true that globalization is characterized by an increasing amount of physical mobility, both elected and forced, its most significant aspect, in terms of culture, is the way in which the complex relations of globalization are transforming localities:

> involving the simultaneous penetration of local worlds by distant forces, and the dislodging of everyday meanings from their "anchors" in the local environment. Embodiment and forces of material circumstances keep most of us, most of the time, situated, but in places that are changing around us and gradually, subtly, losing their power to define the terms of our existence. (Tomlinson 1999: 29)

Although globalization changes or even destroys the conditions which had sustained previous modes of culture, it also supplies new resources for new forms of culture. To see this as a significant cultural development does not mean that we must first embrace the myth of folk culture and see the local as having previously existed in isolation from other localities, global or otherwise. As we saw in chapter 1, there are no such cultures: all cultures have appropriated what was at first "foreign," which was gradually absorbed as "second nature."

Perhaps there will never be a global culture shared horizontally by all peoples of the globe; local circumstances, including local

119

traditions, may always preclude it. But is that the kind of global culture worth working towards? Better, I think, to build a world culture that is not a monoculture, marked only by hierarchical distinctions, but a world culture which values plurality, in which diversity and difference exist in horizontal relations, equally valued as legitimate ways of living our relation to nature (including our own human nature) and, perhaps more important, ways of living our relations to each other. We would all become cosmopolitans, citizens of the world. And, as John Tomlinson (1999: 194) observes, "The first characteristic of cosmopolitanism . . . is a keen grasp of a globalized world as one in which 'there are no others.'" This is not a denial of difference but an insistence on seeing difference within the context of a shared humanity: in effect, to live in both the local and the global and share a "glocalized" culture. This would be a truly popular culture.

Notes

1   Peter Burke (1981: 5) refers to the "discovery" of popular culture in the eighteenth century. Although I understand and fully accept his argument, I use the term "invention" to point to the ways in which popular culture as a concept first emerges in this period. As Burke himself observes, the term was first coined by Johann Gottfried Herder in the 1770s. Therefore, although we are both concerned with popular culture, Burke is interested in the texts and practices of popular culture, whereas my focus is on popular culture as a concept produced by mainly middle-class intellectuals. I am certainly not suggesting that popular culture did not exist until the late eighteenth century; my argument is that it was only in the late eighteenth century that popular culture emerged as an intellectual concept. Therefore, although it is probably the case that there have always been texts and practices and modes of appropriation we could describe as popular culture, the intellectual concept of popular culture is of fairly recent origin.

2   The term folk-lore (later folklore) was introduced into the English language in 1846. In a letter to the *Athenaeum*, W. J. Thoms (writing under the alias Ambrose Merton) proposed that what had previously been known as "popular antiquities" would be better described as "Folk-Lore – the Lore of the People" (1846: 862). A year later Mary Howitt introduced the term folk song (*Howitt's Journal of Literature and Popular Progress*, April 17, 1847). The collecting of songs and stories

was institutionalized with the formation of the the Folk-Lore Society in 1878 (the first International Folk-Lore Congress was held in 1891) and the Folk Song Society in 1898.

3   Their idealization of the peasantry of the past is similar to the post-colonial discourse that can be found in contemporary tourist guides to ancient sites in, for example, Egypt, Greece, or Turkey. *The Lonely Planet Guide to Cairo* (2000: 138), for instance, warns the visitor to the Giza Plateau, "it's difficult to gaze in awe at these ancient wonders with modern Egypt tugging so persistently at your sleeve." Any visitor, we are told, must be prepared "to run the gauntlet of . . . . [the] dollar-driven mob."

4   It was also hoped that the influence of folk music would discourage the singing by the middle class of "parlor ballads." Vaughan Williams, for example, observed "I do not like music-hall songs very much, but with all their blatant vulgarity they are infinitely superior to the inane rubbish which is sung in the modern drawing-room" (quoted in Gammon 1980: 78).

5   In the preface I said that popular culture is a concept of the learned. The Folk Song Society provides an excellent example of this. Active members of the society included the Principal of the Royal Academy of Music, the Director of the Royal College of Music, the professors of music at Oxford and Cambridge, professional musicians, and musical journalists. To ensure that membership remained restricted, prospective members had to be approved by the committee, and members were charged an annual subscription of 10s 6d (Shiach 1989: 130). The Folk Song Society was not somewhere one would expect to meet members of the folk, unless of course they were there as performers of a culture now appropriated by middle-class intellectuals.

Chapter 2: Popular Culture as Mass Culture

1   Greta Jones (1980) also argues that Gobineau's division of the world into black, white, and yellow races, each existing in a fixed hierarchy of racial types and behavior, was derived from his understanding of the social class structure in his native France. The idea that social classes have the characteristics of races was also an idea put forward in 1879 by British historian Alfred Marshall. Although he is in no doubt that

122

the "extension of the English race has been a benefit to the world," he is concerned that

> if the lower classes of Englishmen multiply more rapidly than those which are morally and physically superior, not only will the population of England deteriorate, but also that part of the population of America and Australia which descends from Englishmen will be less intelligent than it otherwise would be. (quoted in Jones 1980: 145)

In 1912 the London Eugenics Education Society published a pamphlet which also insisted that differences of social class were really racial differences: "Taking the population of England in a general sense, the upper classes and the country folk seem, on the whole, to be fairer and taller than the industrial sections of the population." Furthermore, the increasing growth of urbanization and industrialization and, therefore, the increasing growth in the "industrial race," must surely bring about racial disaster, "bearing in mind the characteristics of the two races, the British nation . . . may find themselves becoming darker, shorter, less able to take and keep an initiative, less steadfast and persistent and possibly more emotional" (quoted in Jones 1980: 148–9).

2 Writing at about the same time (1939), but across the Atlantic in the USA, modernist art critic Clement Greenberg (1986: 12) paints much the same picture. Instead of mass culture, he uses the term "kitsch":

> Kitsch is a product of the industrial revolution which urbanized the masses of Western Europe and America and established what is called universal literacy . . . Losing . . . their taste for the folk culture whose background was the countryside, and discovering a new capacity for boredom at the same time, the new urban masses set up a pressure on society to provide them with a kind of culture fit for their own consumption. To fill this demand of the new market, a new commodity was devised: ersatz culture, kitsch, destined for those who, insensible to the values of genuine culture, are hungry nevertheless for the diversion that culture of some sort can provide.

Kitsch, Greenberg maintains, "welcomes and cultivates this insensibil-ity"; it operates by "formulas," providing "vicarious experiences and faked sensations"; it "changes according to style, but always remains the same" as "predigested art," requiring little effort to consume and provides "a short cut to the pleasure of art that detours what is necessarily difficult in genuine art" (12, 16, 17).

3 The Frankfurt School was certainly not alone on the political Left in thinking in this way. The Scottish poet Edwin Muir noted this tendency in much left-wing writing of the 1930s:

> the literature of the left is in danger of being dehumanised, formal-ised, throttled by an automatic ideology, which denies humanity except in great bulk, so huge that it has no immediate relation to our lives: the "masses", for instance, not as a collection of men and women, but as an instrument, dehumanised as an army. (letter to Stephen Spender in 1937; quoted in Carey 1992: 39)

Chapter 3: Popular Culture as the "Other" of High Culture

1 The imbeddedness of Shakespeare in working-class culture in nineteenth-century Britain is demonstrated by the fact that the Chartist newspaper, the *Northern Star*, thought it worthwhile to run a series of articles in the spring of 1840 called "Chartism from Shakespeare," in which passages from Shakespeare's plays are used to support the principles and policies of Chartism (Janowitz 1998).

2 For a more detailed account of the changing status of opera, see Storey 2002 and 2003.

3 The classic repertoire begins with Mozart in the 1780s and ends with Puccini in 1926.

4 On the Metropolitan Opera's opening night on October 22, 1883, a contemporary newspaper estimated that the boxes were occupied by people whose wealth was in the region of 540,000,000 dollars (Kolodin 1936: 5). The following evening the *New York Evening Post* commented: "From an artistic and musical point of view, the large boxes in the Metropolitan are a decided mistake. But as the house was avowedly built for social purposes rather than artistic, it is useless to complain about this" (12).

Another measure of the success of the appropriation of opera by social elites can be seen in an article published in the *Atlantic Monthly* in 1916:

> Opera is controlled by a few rich men . . . It does not exist for the good of the whole city, but rather for those with plethoric purses . . . [Opera houses] surround themselves with an exotic atmosphere in which the normal person finds difficulty in breathing . . . they are too little related to the community. (quoted in Levine 1988: 101)

Two years earlier the *Atlantic Review* had published an article in which it was hoped that the increasing popularity of cinema might bring about a situation in which "the art of the stage may escape from the proletariat, and *again* truly belong to those who in larger, finer sense are 'the great ones of the earth'" (207; my italics).

5 The sacralization of culture was an indispensable aspect of the making of cultural exclusivity. In the early twentieth century Benjamin Ives Gilman, secretary to the Boston Museum of Fine Art, could declare without fear of contradiction, that "a museum of art is in essence a temple" (155).

Chapter 4: Popular Culture as an Arena of Hegemony

1 Here is a banal example of how the process operates. Think of the "moral and intellectual leadership" that is necessary to make workable instructions like "Keep Off the Grass" or "No Smoking." Although both are supported by the threat of coercion, they work mainly through the building of a consensus around the necessity for each injunction.

2 There are, of course, limits to negotiations and concessions. As Gramsci makes clear, they can never be allowed to challenge the economic fundamentals of class power. In times of crisis, when moral and intellectual leadership is not enough to secure continued authority, the processes of hegemony are replaced, temporarily, by the coercive power of the "repressive state apparatus": the army, the police, the prison system, etc.

3 Working within the framework of hegemony, Hall deploys the concept of "articulation" (Hall 1985, 1996a) to explain the processes of ideological struggle. Hall's use plays on the term's double meaning to express and connect: first, the process is an "articulation" in that meaning has to be expressed (the "text" has to be made to signify); second, it is an "articulation" in that meaning is always expressed in a specific context (connected to another context the "text" could be made to signify something quite different). A "text," therefore, is not the issuing source of meaning, but a site where the articulation of meaning – variable meaning(s) – can be made. And because "texts" are "multi-accentual" (Volosinov 1973), they can be articulated with different "accents" by different people in different contexts for different politics. In this way, then, meaning, and the field of culture more generally, is always a site of negotiation and conflict.

4 The problem with some modes of cultural analysis which present themselves as "political" is that the only role allocated to the working class (or any other oppressed or exploited group) is that of victims of "false consciousness." Jesus Martin-Barbero (1993: 68–9) refers to "the twisting of meaning which has converted Marx's often quoted affirmation – the dominant ideas of a period are the ideas of the dominant classes – into a justification of a class ethnocentrism in which the dominated classes have no ideas and are not capable of producing ideas." In this way, ordinary people are subjected to a "double oppression": oppressed both by capitalism and those accounts of capitalism which seek to undermine it. This is not to deny exploitation and oppression, but it is to deny that the lives of "ordinary" people consist of nothing but, and are totally defined by, exploitation and oppression. This way of thinking has become so deeply ingrained in Left cultural analysis that to suggest that ordinary people are in any way capable of acting as other than cultural dupes is to be dismissed as a cultural populist.

There is something rather ridiculous about the idea that cultural domination is a simple process in which the culture industries send out ideologically charged commodities to be consumed whole by unsuspecting and increasingly manipulated masses. This is a world without conflict or contradiction, in which there is total compliance from both those who produce the commodities and those who consume them. Against this, I would want to insist that culture is not just a space of manipulation but is also where we discover possibilities, where we struggle, negotiate, have fun, as we make sense of who we are, where we are, and who and where we would like to be.

Chapter 5: Popular Culture as Postmodern Culture

1 One key factor is identified by a correspondent to the magazine *Opera* (December 1990), who observed: "[In 1962] as an articled clerk on £17 a week, I could afford, and sat regularly in the balcony stall sides [in the Royal Opera House, Covent Garden] at 10/6d [about 52p]. Today at £48, such a seat would require a gross salary of £80,820. Some articled clerk!" (quoted in Evans 1999: 139). For more details, see Storey 2002 and 2003.

Chapter 6: Popular Culture as the "Roots" and "Routes" of Cultural Identities

1 Identities are also always a compromise between nature and culture; between what we desire to do and what nature (including our own biology) allows us to do. Although it is undoubtedly true that nature (including our own nature) is fashioned by our culture, it is also true that the fashioning of nature (including our own nature) is always within conditions already established by nature.

2 Sigmund Freud (1991) also saw the importance of recognizing that memory is always situated in the present. Working almost like a historian of the self, he developed a clinical practice, the purpose of which was to stop the past causing pain in the present. Because what is remembered is not the past, but a representation of the past, the pain of memory is made and remade in the present. Therefore, it is not a question of forgetting, but of learning to interpret memories in ways which no longer threaten happiness in the present and the future.

3 To think that memory is something embodied in certain objects is perhaps to be guilty of a kind of "memory fetishism." That is, what is humanly produced – memories – are seen to exist outside the

127

human, to take on a life of their own, a life which is other than the life which gave them an existence. This line of thinking is very similar to Marx's notion of commodity fetishism. What he said about religion, to explain the fetishism of commodities, is an apt description of what I am calling memory fetishism, "the products of the human brain appear as autonomous figures endowed with a life of their own" (1976: 165).

4 I have not commented on Lacan's theory of the Oedipus crisis, because to do so would have diverted me from my specific purpose. For an excellent account of the Oedipus crisis (and Lacan's work more generally), see Evans 1996.

5 In the light of my endorsement of Halbwachs' theory of memory, I think I should make clear the management of my own remembering. Although what I remember is true, it is certainly ordered by what I now know about fan culture.

Chapter 7: Popular Culture as Popular or Mass Art

1 Simon Frith (1998) and John Street (2000) have argued that aesthetics is something to which cultural studies should pay more attention. Although I value their interventions, both very quickly blur the distinction between aesthetic value and other forms of evaluation. While I agree that academics have "a duty to make (rather than evade) value judgements when teaching popular culture" (Frith 1998: 8), and when teaching everything else besides, questions of value do not have to be questions of aesthetic value.

2 Carroll's main focus is the distinction between avant-garde and mass art. However, as he himself concedes: "where I invoke the notion of 'high art' . . . I mean it to be understood primarily in terms of the avant-garde" (208). His use of "primarily" rather than exclusively allows me to broaden his distinction to one between high art and mass art.

3 Something similar is happening when we see terms like black writer, female writer, gay writer, working-class writer. Such terms may enlarge what counts as writing, but they do so at the expense of keeping in place the unmarked and normative idea of the writer as white, male, heterosexual, and middle-class.

Chapter 8: Popular Culture as Global Culture

1   The fact that the former Beatle George Harrison requested that his ashes be scattered in the sacred River Ganges is perhaps a telling example of the influence of the east on the west.

2   The global economic status of Hong Kong, South Korea, Singapore, and especially Japan certainly problematizes any straightforward idea of globalization as Americanization. As David Morley (1996: 349) observes, "modernity (or perhaps postmodernity) may perhaps in future be located more in the Pacific than the Atlantic." Similarly, the idea of Americanization looks rather different when we consider the fact that the United States has the third largest Hispanic population in the world, and that it is estimated that by 2076 (the tercentennial of the American Revolution) people of Native American, African, Asian, or Latin descent will make up the majority of its population (335).

3   In order to make money – and the making of money is not in dispute – companies like McDonalds have to reach subtle compromises with the cuisine and the customs of the localities in which they operate. Eating at McDonalds in Cyprus is different from eating at McDonalds in, say, England. Drinking beer (as you can in Cyprus) completely changes the potential meaning of the experience by undermining the idea of "fast food."

4   George Ritzer (1999: 89), however, makes this point: "while we will continue to see global diversity, many, most, perhaps eventually all of those cultures will be affected by American exports; America will become virtually everyone's 'second culture'."

5   A more benign example of the insistence on "roots" is the explosive growth in family history research in both Britain and the US. Globalization may be driving the search for "roots" in, or perhaps for "routes" back into, a more secure past in the hope of stabilizing identities in the present.

References

Adorno, Theodor, and Horkheimer, Max, 1979. *Dialectic of Enlightenment*. London: Verso. [First published in 1947.]

Althusser, Louis, 1998. "Ideology and Ideological State Apparatuses." In John Storey (ed.), *Cultural Theory and Popular Culture: A Reader*, 2nd edn. London: Prentice Hall, 153–64.

Ang, Ien, 1996. *Living Room Wars: Rethinking Media Audiences for a Postmodern World*. London: Routledge.

Arnold, Matthew, 1896. *Letters 1848–1888*, ed. George W. E. Russell. 2 vols. London: Macmillan.

—— 1954. *Poetry and Prose*, London: Rupert Hart-Davis.

—— 1960. *Culture and Anarchy*, Cambridge: Cambridge University Press.

—— 1973. *On Education*, Harmondsworth: Penguin.

—— 1977. *Complete Works*, volume 5. Ann Arbor: University of Michigan Press.

Ash, Russell, 2001. *The Top Ten of Everything*. London: Penguin.

Bartlett, Frederic, 1967. *Remembering: A Study in Experimental and Social Psychology*. Cambridge: Cambridge University Press.

Baudrillard, Jean, 1983. *Simulations*, trans. Paul Foss. New York: Semiotext(e).

Bourdieu, Pierre, 1984. *Distinction: A Critique of the Judgment of Taste*, trans. Paul Patton. Cambridge, MA: Harvard University Press.

—— 1993. *The Field of Cultural Production*, trans. Philip Richard Nice. Cambridge: Polity.

Braund, Simon, 1999. "Check out the figure baby." *Empire Movie Magazine*, September.

References

Brooker, Peter, and Brooker, Will, 1997a. "Introduction." In Peter Brooker and Will Brooker (eds.), *Postmodern After-Images*. London: Edward Arnold, 1–19.

—— 1997b. "Styles of Pluralism." In Peter Brooker and Will Brooker (eds.), *Postmodern After-Images*. London: Edward Arnold, 55–9.

Burke, Peter, 1981. "People's History or Total History." In Raphael Samuel (ed.), *People's History and Socialist Thought*. London: Routledge & Kegan Paul, 4–15.

—— 1992. "We, the People: Popular Culture and Popular Identity in Modern Europe." In Scott Lash and Jonathan Friedman (eds.), *Modernity and Identity*. Oxford: Blackwell, 293–308.

—— 1996. *Popular Culture in Early Modern Europe*, revised reprint. Aldershot: Scolar Press.

Butler, Judith, 1998. "Merely Cultural." *New Left Review*, 227, 33–44.

—— 1999. *Gender Trouble: Feminism and the Subversion of Identity*. New York: Routledge.

Carey, John, 1992. *The Intellectuals and the Masses: Pride and Prejudice among the Literary Intelligentsia, 1880–1939*. London: Faber and Faber.

Carroll, Noel, 1998. *A Philosophy of Mass Art*. Oxford: Clarendon Press.

Certeau, Michel de, 1984. *The Practice of Everyday Life*, trans. Steven Rendall. Berkeley: University of California Press.

Chaney, David, 1994. *The Cultural Turn*. London: Routledge.

Chartier, Roger, 1993. "Popular Culture: A Concept Revisited." *Intellectual History Newsletter*, 15, 3–13.

Clark, Robert T., Jr. 1969. *Herder: His Life and Thought*. Berkeley: University of California Press.

Clarke, John, Hall, Stuart, Jefferson, Tony, and Roberts, Brian, 1976. "Subcultures, Cultures and Class." In Stuart Hall and Tony Jefferson (eds.), *Resistance Through Rituals: Youth Subcultures in Post-war Britain*. London: Hutchinson, 9–74.

Cohen, Gillian, 1996. *Memory in the Real World*, 2nd edn. Hove: Psychology Press.

Collins, Jim, 1989. *Uncommon Cultures: Popular Culture and Post-Modernism*. New York: Routledge.

—— 1992. "Postmodernism and Television." In Robert C. Allen (ed.), *Channels of Discourse, Reassembled*. Routledge: London, 327–53.

131

—— 1993. "Genericity in the Nineties: Eclectic Irony and the New Sincerity." In J. Collins, H. Radner, A. Preacher Collins (eds.), *Film Theory Goes to the Movies*. Routledge: London, 242–63.

Denning, Michael, 1987. *Mechanic Accents: Dime Novels and Working-Class Culture*. London: Verso.

DiMaggio, Paul, 1992. "Cultural Boundaries and Structural Change: The Extension of the High Culture Model to Theater, Opera, and the Dance, 1900–1940." In Michèle Lamont and Marcel Fournier (eds.), *Cultivating Differences: Symbolic Boundaries and the Making of Inequality*. Chicago: University of Chicago Press, 21–57.

—— 1998. "Cultural Entrepreneurship in Nineteenth-Century Boston: The Creation of an Organizational Base for High Culture in America." In John Storey (ed.), *Cultural Theory and Popular Culture: A Reader*, 2nd edn. Hemel Hempstead: Prentice Hall, 454–75.

Docker, John, 1994. *Postmodernism and Popular Culture*. Cambridge: Cambridge University Press.

Dorson, Richard M., 1968. *History of British Folklore*, vol. 1. London: Routledge.

Du Gay, Paul, Hall, Stuart, Janes, Linda, Mackay, Hugh, and Negus, Keith, 1997. *Doing Cultural Studies: The Story of the Sony Walkman*. London: Sage.

Duncan, Andrew, 1999. "The Andrew Duncan Interview: Mike Myers." *Radio Times*, 31 July–6 August.

Eagleton, Terry, 1983. *Literary Theory: An Introduction*. Oxford: Blackwell.

Eliot, T. S., 1948. *Notes Towards the Definition of Culture*. London: Faber.

Evans, David T., 1999. *Phantasmagoria: A Sociology of Opera*. Aldershot: Ashgate.

Evans, Dylan, 1996. *An Introductory Dictionary of Lacanian Psychoanalysis*. London: Routledge.

Featherstone, Mike, 1991. *Consumer Culture & Postmodernism*. London: Sage.

Ferguson, Marjorie, and Golding, Peter, 1997. "Cultural Studies and Changing Times: An Introduction." In Marjorie Ferguson and Peter Golding (eds.), *Cultural Studies in Question*. London: Sage, xiii–xxvii.

Fiske, John, 1989. *Reading the Popular*. Boston, MA: Unwin Hyman.

Floyd, Nigel, 1999. "Shagadelic Sequel." *SFX Magazine*, September.

Foucault, Michel, 1982. "What is Enlightenment?" trans. Catherine Porter. In Paul Rabinow (ed.), *The Foucault Reader*. Harmondsworth: Peregrine.

References

Freud, Sigmund, 1991. *Introductory Lectures on Psychoanalysis*. Harmonds-worth: Penguin. [First published in 1963.]

Frith, Simon, 1996. *Performing Rites: Evaluating Popular Music*. Oxford: Oxford University Press.

Gammon, Vic, 1980. "Folk Song Collecting in Sussex and Surrey, 1843–1914." *History Workshop Journal*, 15, 61–89.

Garnham, Nicholas, 1998. "Political Economy and Cultural Studies: Recon-ciliation or Divorce." In John Storey (ed.), *Cultural Theory and Popular Culture: A Reader*, 2nd edn. Hemel Hempstead: Prentice Hall, 600–12.

Gillespie, Marie, 1995. *Television, Ethnicity and Cultural Change*. London: Routledge.

Golding, Peter, and Murdoch, Graham, 1991. "Culture, Communication and Political Economy." In John Curran and Michael Gurevitch (eds.), *Mass Media and Society*. London: Arnold, 15–32.

Goodwin, Andrew, 1991. "Popular Music and Postmodern Theory." In *Cultural Studies*, 5:2, 173–88.

Gramsci, Antonio, 1971. *Selections from Prison Notebooks*, ed. and trans. Quintin Hoare and Geoffrey Nowell Smith. London: Lawrence & Wishart.

—— 1998. "Hegemony, Intellectuals and the State." In John Storey (ed.), *Cultural Theory and Popular Culture: A Reader*, 2nd edn. London: Prentice Hall, 210–16.

Greenberg, Clement, 1965. "The Modernist Painter." *Art and Literature*, 4, 193–201.

—— 1986. "Avant-Garde and Kitsch." In *The Collected Essays and Criti-cism, volume 1: Perceptions and Judgments 1939–1944*, Chicago: University of Chicago Press, 5–22.

Grossberg, Lawrence, 1988. *It's a Sin: Essays on Postmodernism, Politics and Culture*, Sydney: Power Publications.

—— 1992. *We Gotta Get Out of this Place: Popular Conservatism and Post-modern Culture*, New York and London: Routledge.

—— 1998. "Cultural Studies vs Political Economy: Is Anybody Else Bored with this Debate?" In John Storey (ed.), *Cultural Theory and Popular Culture: A Reader*, 2nd edn. Hemel Hempstead: Prentice Hall, 613–24.

Grossberg, Lawrence, Nelson, Cary, Treichler, Paula A. (eds.) 1992. *Cultural Studies*. New York and London: Routledge.

Guinness Book of Records, 2001. London: Guinness World Records.

References

Halbwachs, Maurice, 1980. *The Collective Memory*, trans. Francis J. Ditter Jr. and Vida Yazdi Ditter. New York: Harper and Row.

Hall, Stuart, 1980. "Encoding/Decoding." In Stuart Hall, Dorothy Hobson, Andrew Lowe, and Paul Willis (eds.), *Culture, Media, Language*. London: Hutchinson, 128–38.

—— 1985. "The Rediscovery of Ideology: The Return of the Repressed in Media Studies." In Veronica Beechey and James Donald (eds.), *Subjectivity and Social Relations*. Milton Keynes: Open University Press, 23–55.

—— 1992a. "Cultural Studies and its Theoretical Legacies." In Lawrence Grossberg, Cary Nelson, Paula A. Treichler (eds.), *Cultural Studies*. New York: Routledge, 277–94.

—— 1992b. "The Question of Cultural Identity." In Stuart Hall and Tony McGrew (eds.), *Modernity and Its Futures*, Cambridge: Polity Press, 273–323.

—— 1996a. "On Postmodernism and Articulation." In David Morley and Chen Kuan-Hsing (eds.), *Stuart Hall: Critical Dialogues in Cultural Studies*. London: Routledge, 131–50.

—— 1996b. "Cultural Studies: Two Paradigms." In John Storey (ed.), *What is Cultural Studies? A Reader*. London: Edward Arnold, 31–48.

—— 1996c. "When was 'the Post-Colonial'? Thinking at the Limit." In Iain Chambers and Lidia Curti (eds.), *The Post-Colonial Question*. London: Routledge, 242–60.

—— 1996d. "The Problem of Ideology: Marxism without Guarantees." In David Morley and Chen Kuan-Hsing (eds.), *Stuart Hall: Critical Dialogues in Cultural Studies*. London: Routledge, 25–46.

—— 1996e. "Who Needs Identity?" In Stuart Hall and Paul du Gay (eds.), *Questions of Cultural Identity*. London: Sage, 1–17.

—— 1997. "The Work of Representation." In Stuart Hall (ed.), *Representation: Cultural Representations and Signifying Practices*. London: Sage, 13–64.

—— 1998. "Notes on Deconstructing 'the Popular'." In John Storey (ed.), *Cultural Theory and Popular Culture: A Reader*, 2nd edn. Hemel Hempstead: Prentice Hall, 442–53.

Hall, Stuart, and Whannel, Paddy, 1964. *The Popular Arts*. London: Hutchinson.

Harker, Dave, 1985. *Fakesong: The Manufacture of British Folksong, 1700 to the Present Day*. Milton Keynes: Open University Press.

References

Hart, Walter Morris, 1906. "Professor Child and the Ballad." *Proceedings of the Modern Languages Association of America*, XXI: 4, 755–807.

Harvey, David, 1990. *The Condition of Postmodernity*. London: Blackwell.

Hebdige, Dick, 1998. "Postmodernism and 'The Other Side'." In John Storey (ed.), *Cultural Theory and Popular Culture: A Reader*. Hemel Hempstead: Prentice Hall, 371–86.

Hoggart, Richard, 1990. *The Uses of Literacy*. Harmondsworth: Penguin. [First published in 1957.]

Huyssen, Andreas, 1986. *After the Great Divide: Modernism, Mass Culture and Postmodernism*. Basingstoke: Macmillan.

Jameson, Fredric, 1983. "Postmodernism and Consumer Society." In Hal Foster (ed.), *Post-Modern Culture*, London: Pluto Press, 111–25.

—— 1984. "Postmodernism, or the Cultural Logic of Late Capitalism." *New Left Review*, 146, 53–93.

—— 1988. "The Politics of Theory: Ideological Positions in the Postmodernism Debate." In Fredric Jameson, *The Ideologies of Theory: Essays*, vol. 2. London: Routledge, 103–13.

Janowitz, Anne, 1998. *Lyric and Labour in the Romantic Tradition*. Cambridge: Cambridge University Press.

Jenkins, Henry, 1992. *Textual Poachers*. London: Routledge.

Johnson, Richard, 1996. "What is Cultural Studies anyway?" In John Storey (ed.), *What is Cultural Studies? A Reader*. London: Edward Arnold, 75–114.

Jones, Greta, 1980. *Social Darwinism and English Thought: The Interaction between Biological and Social Theory*. Sussex: Harvester Press.

Kolodin, Irving, 1936. *The Metropolitan Opera 1883–1935*. New York: Oxford University Press.

Kristeva, Julia, 1989. *Tales of Love*, trans. Leon S. Roudiez. New York: Columbia University Press.

Lacan, Jacques, 1977. *Ecrits: A Selection*, trans. Alan Sheridan. London: Tavistock.

Landsberg, Alison, 1995. "Prosthetic Memory: Total Recall and Blade Runner." *Body & Society*, 1:3/4, 175–89.

Leavis, F. R., 1933. *For Continuity*. Cambridge: Minority Press.

—— 1998. "Mass Civilisation and Minority Culture." In John Storey (ed.), *Cultural Theory and Popular Culture: A Reader*, 2nd edn. Hemel Hempstead: Prentice Hall, 13–21. [First published in 1933.]

References

Leavis, F. R., and Thompson, Denys, 1977. *Culture and Environment*. Westport, CT: Greenwood Press. [First published in 1933.]

Leavis, Q. D., 1978. *Fiction and the Reading Public*. London: Chatto and Windus. [First published in 1932.]

Levine, Lawrence W., 1988. *Highbrow/Lowbrow: The Emergence of Cultural Hierarchy in America*. Cambridge, MA: Harvard University Press.

Liebes, Tamar, and Katz, Elihu, 1993. *The Export of Meaning: Cross-cultural Readings of Dallas*, 2nd edn. Cambridge: Polity Press.

Loftus, Elisabeth F., 1996. *Eyewitness Testimony*, Cambridge, MA: Harvard University Press.

Lovell, Terry, 1998. "Cultural Production." In John Storey (ed.), *Cultural Theory and Popular Culture: A Reader*, 2nd edn. Hemel Hempstead: Prentice Hall, 476–82.

Lyotard, Jean-François, 1984. *The Postmodern Condition*, trans. Geoffrey Bennington and Brian Massumi. Manchester: Manchester University Press.

McConachie, Bruce A., 1988. "New York Operagoing, 1825–50: Creating an Elite Social Ritual." *American Music*, 6, 181–92.

Macdonald, Dwight, 1998. "A Theory of Mass Culture." In John Storey (ed.), *Cultural Theory and Popular Culture: A Reader*, 2nd edn. Hemel Hempstead: Prentice Hall, 22–36.

McLuhan, Marshall, 1967. *Understanding Media*. London: Sphere, 1967.

McRobbie, Angela, 1996. "Looking Back at New Times and its Critics." In David Morley and Chen Kuan-Hsing (eds.), *Stuart Hall: Critical Dialogues in Cultural Studies*. London: Routledge, 238–61.

Marcuse, Herbert, 1968. *One-Dimensional Man*. London: Sphere. [First published in 1964.]

Martin-Barbero, Jesus, 1993. *Communication, Culture and Hegemony*. London: Sage.

Marx, Karl, 1976. *Capital*, volume I. Harmondsworth: Penguin. [First published in 1867.]

Marx, Karl, 1977. *The Eighteenth Brumaire of Louis Bonaparte*. Moscow: Progress Publishers. [First published in 1852.]

Massey, Doreen, 1994. *Space, Place and Gender*. Cambridge: Polity.

Merton, Ambrose (alias of W. J. Thoms), 1846. "Letter." *Athenaeum*, 22 August.

Michaelis-Jena, Ruth, 1970. *The Brothers Grimm*, London: Routledge & Kegan Paul.

136

References

Morley, David, 1996. "UurAm, Modernity, Reason and Alterity; or, Postmodernism, the Highest Stage of Cultural Imperialism." In David Morley and Kuan-Hsing Chen (eds.), *Stuart Hall: Critical Dialogues in Cultural Studies*. London: Routledge, 326–60.

—— 1997. "Theoretical Orthodoxies: Textualism, Constructivism and the 'New Ethnography' in Cultural Studies." In Marjorie Ferguson and Peter Golding (eds.), *Cultural Studies in Question*. London: Sage, 121–37.

Nava, Mica, 1987. "Consumerism and its Contradictions." *Cultural Studies*, 1:2, 204–10.

Nederveen Pieterse, Jan, 1995. "Globalisation as Hybridisation." *International Sociology*, 9:2, 161–84.

Nora, Pierre, 1989. "Between Memory and History: Les lieux de mémoire." *Representations*, 26, 7–24.

Ortega y Gasset, José, 1961. *The Revolt of the Masses*. London: George Allen & Unwin. [First published in 1930.]

—— 1968. *The Dehumanization of Art*, trans. Helen Weyl. Princeton, NJ: Princeton University Press. [First published in 1948.]

Palmer, Martyn, 1999. "Oooh . . . Eye Say." In *Inside Film: Austin Powers: The Spy Who Shagged Me*. Blackstar.co.uk.

Parry, Hubert, 1899. "Inaugural Address." *Journal of the Folk Song Society*, 1:1, 1–3.

Peterson, Richard A., 1992. "Understanding Audience Segmentation: From elite and mass to omnivore and univore." *Poetics*, 21, 243–58.

Peterson, Richard A., and Kern, Roger M., 1996. "Changing Highbrow Taste: From Snob to Omnivore." *American Sociological Review*, 61, 900–7.

Peterson Richard A., and Simkus, Albert, 1992. "How Musical Tastes Mark Occupational Status Groups." In Michèle Lamont and Marcel Fournier (eds.), *Cultivating Difference: Symbolic Boundaries and the Making of Inequality*, Chicago: University of Chicago Press, 152–86.

Raynor, Harry, 1972. *A Social History of Music: From the Middle Ages to Beethoven*. London: Barrie & Jenkins.

Ritzer, George, 1999. *The McDonaldization Thesis*. London: Sage.

Robertson, Roland, 1995. "Glocalization: Time–Space and Homogeneity–Heterogeneity." In Mike Featherstone, Scott Lash, and Robert Robertson (eds.), *Global Modernities*. London: Sage, 25–44.

Said, Edward, 1993. *Culture and Imperialism*. New York: Vintage Books.

References

Schiller, Herbert, 1979. "Transnational Media and National Development."
In K. Nordenstreng and Herbert Schiller (eds.), *National Sovereignty and
International Communication*, Norwood, NJ: Ablex, 21–32.

Sharp, Cecil J., 1907. *English Folk-Song: Some Conclusions*. London: Novello.

Shiach, Morag, 1989. *Discourse on Popular Culture*. Cambridge: Polity Press.

Shusterman, Richard, 1992. *Pragmatic Aesthetics: Living Beauty, Rethinking
Art*. Oxford: Blackwell.

Smith, Barbara Herrnstein, 1988. *Contingencies of Value: Alternative Perspectives for Critical Theory*. Cambridge, MA: Harvard University Press.

Sontag, Susan, 1966. *Against Interpretation*, New York: Dell.

Stocking, George W., Jr., 1968. *Race, Culture, and Evolution: Essays in the
History of Anthropology*. New York: Free Press.

Storey, John, 1985. "Matthew Arnold: The Politics of an Organic Intellectual." *Literature and History*, 11:2, 217–28.

—— 1999. *Cultural Consumption and Everyday Life*. London: Arnold.

—— 2001. *Cultural Theory and Popular Culture*, 3rd edn. Harlow: Pearson
Education.

—— 2002. "'Expecting Rain': Opera as Popular Culture?" In Jim Collins
(ed.), *High-Pop: Making Culture into Popular Entertainment*. Oxford:
Blackwell, 32–55.

—— (2003). "The Social Life of Opera." *European Journal of Cultural Studies*,
6:1, 5–35.

Street, John, 2000. "Aesthetics, Policy and the Politics of Popular Culture." *European Journal of Cultural Studies*, 3:1, 27–43.

Sturken, Marita, 1997. *Tangled Memories: The Vietnam War, the AIDS Epi-
demic, and the Politics of Remembering*. Berkeley: University of California
Press.

Tomlinson, John, 1997. "Internationalism, Globalization and Cultural Imperialism." In Kenneth Thompson (ed.), *Media and Regulation*. London:
Sage, 117–62.

—— 1999. *Globalization and Culture*. Cambridge: Polity Press.

Turner, Bryan S., 1987. "A Note on Nostalgia." *Theory, Culture & Society*,
4, 147–56.

Volosinov, Valentin, 1973. *Marxism and the Philosophy of Language*. New
York: Seminar Press.

Williams, Raymond, 1958a. "Culture is ordinary." In Norman McKenzie
(ed.), *Conviction*. London: MacGibbon and Kee, 74–92.

—— 1958b. "Fiction and the Writing Public." *Essays in Criticism*, 7, 426–7.

—— 1993. *Culture and Society*. London: Hogarth Press. [First published in 1958.]

—— 1998. "The Analysis of Culture." In John Storey (ed.), *Cultural Theory and Popular Culture: A Reader*, 2nd edn. Hemel Hempstead: Prentice Hall, 48–56.

Willis, Paul, 1990. *Common Culture*. Milton Keynes: Open University Press.

Wilson, Elizabeth, 1998. "Fashion and Postmodernism." In John Storey (ed.), *Cultural Theory and Popular Culture: A Reader*. Hemel Hempstead: Prentice Hall, 392–402.

Wolff, Janet, 1989. "The Ideology of Autonomous Art." In Richard Leppert and Susan McClary (eds.), *Music and Society: The Politics of Composition, Performance and Reception*. Cambridge: Cambridge University Press, 1–12.

Wordsworth, William, 1999. "Advertisement" [1798]. In William Wordsworth and Samuel Taylor Coleridge, *Lyrical Ballads*. Harmondsworth: Penguin, v–vi.

—— 1973. "Preface to Lyrical Ballads (1802)." In Harold Bloom and Lionel Trilling (eds.), *Romantic Poetry and Prose*. Oxford: Oxford University Press, 594–611.

Young, Robert J. C., 1995. *Colonial Desire: Hybridity in Theory, Culture and Race*. London: Routledge.

Zelechow, Bernard, 1993. "The Opera: The Meeting of Popular and Elite Culture in the Nineteenth Century." *History of European Ideas*, 16, 261–6.

Index

access to culture 53–4
acid perspectivism 65
Adam Adamant 67
Adams, Williams 86
Adorno, Theodor 27–8, 29, 30, 100
advertising 74, 101
aesthetics 92, 105, 128n1
agency 51, 55, 60, 72–3, 93
Alloway, Lawrence 63
allusion 67
Althusser, Louis 50, 80–1
Americanization 109–12, 113–14, 129n2
Ang, Ien 112–13, 114
Angel Heart 66
"Anyone Who Had A Heart" (Springfield) 89–90
appropriation of culture 53–4, 55
Arena 36
Arnold, Matthew: barbarians/ philistines/populace 18–20; culture ix, 58, 63; *Culture and Anarchy* 16–21; mass culture 16–17; as organic intellectual 50; tradition 93; working class 23
art: autonomy 100; entertainment 74, 76–7; legitimacy 94; market economy 42; modernism 42; Ortega y Gasset 42; production 100; sacralization 33
art (types): avant-garde 95, 128n2; high 128n2; mass 95–6, 97, 102, 128n2; popular 101, 102–3
articulation 72–3, 126n3
Ash, Russell 96
Atlantic Monthly 125n4
Atlantic Review 125n4
Atomic Kitten, "Whole Again" 88
attitudes 60
audience 28, 95–6
audience studies 61–2
Austin Powers: The Spy Who Shagged Me 67, 73
Australian Aborigines 98
authenticity 51, 116–17
authorial intention 98
authority 22–3, 30, 41
autonomy 100

Back to the Future I, II, and *III* 66
ballads 2, 5
Barnum, P. T. 37
Bartlett, Frederic 84
Baudrillard, Jean 64
Beatles 63, 129n1

Birmingham University: Centre for Contemporary Cultural Studies 104
Blue Velvet 66
Boston: elite 33–4; high culture 32–4; middle class 34; Museum of Fine Arts 33, 125n5
Boston Symphony Orchestra 33
Boswell, James 8
Bourdieu, Pierre 43, 44, 94, 100, 105
Braund, Simon 73
bricolage 70–1, 72
British colonialism 49
Brooker, Peter 71
Brooker, Will 71
Burke, Peter 1, 4, 8, 121n1
Butler, Judith 62, 91

canon 21–2, 92, 94
capitalism: commodities 57; cultural studies 59; entrepreneurship 50; high culture 64; popular culture 51; profit 56–7
capitalism, late 65
Carey, John 14–15, 41
Caribbean 49
Carroll, Noel 95, 97, 128n2
Centre for Contemporary Cultural Studies (Birmingham) 104
Certeau, Michel de 90
Chaney, David 70
Chartier, Roger xi
Child, Francis James 2, 5
Christian Broadcasting Network 72–3
cinema *see* film
civilization: culture 22; education 20; folk song 12–13; opera 39; race 18, 25–6; savages/peasantry 6–8
Clark, Robert T. jr. 4
Clarke, John 61
classification 32–3, 43–4
Clodd, Edward 7

Cohen, Gillian 84
Collins, Jim: articulation 72–3; bricolage 70–1, 72; hyperconscious intertextuality 72; recycling 71–2
colonialism 49, 115–16
commodification 68–9
commodities: access 56; capitalism 57; cultural consumption 54–5; cultural studies 58; culture 110, 112; culture industry 27–8, 52, 126–7n4; fetishism 128n3; global culture 109–10; United States of America 112
communication 87
community: diasporic 61; organic 23
comprehension, ease of 95–6
conformity 27–8
consciousness: culture industry 28–9; false 28, 56, 111, 126n4; hyperconsciousness 72
consensus 49, 56, 125n1
consumerism 61
consumption: cultural studies 53, 58; identity 78–9, 89; mass culture 100; opera 77; passivity 52–3, 111; pop music 89–90; popular culture 97–8; production 57, 60, 79, 83, 89; re-creative 61; taste 97; *see also* cultural consumption
cosmopolitanism 120
cuisine 108
cultural analysis 55–6, 60
cultural consumption 43, 44, 47, 54–5, 78–9
cultural imperialism 108
cultural pessimism 68
cultural studies ix; aesthetics 128n1; audience studies 61–2; capitalism 59; commodities 58; consumption 53, 58; economic determinism 57–8; ethnography 61–2; Gramsci

cultural studies (*cont'd*)
  xi, 58; hegemony 53; high culture
  93–4; political economy 61–2;
  politics 62, 126n4; *The Popular Arts*
  102–3; production 60
culture ix–x; Arnold ix, 58, 63;
  attitudes 60; authority 41;
  civilization 22; commodities 110,
  112; education 27; elite 17–18,
  21–2, 30, 41; evaluation 104–5;
  exclusivity 43; flows 115;
  globalization 120; Gramsci 61;
  hegemony 111; hierarchy 49,
  92; hybridization 108, 115, 117,
  118–19; identity 81–2, 88;
  imports 115–16; legitimacy 105;
  modernism 32, 41; politics 124n3;
  postmodernism 72–3; power xi,
  48, 54, 62, 92, 94, 101, 106;
  production/reproduction 43,
  53–4; sacralization 125n5; social
  class 10–11, 17–18, 26, 43,
  44–7; valorization 100–1;
  Williams xii; working class
  10–11, 14, 20
culture industry: commodities 27–8,
  52, 126–7n4; conformity 27–8;
  consciousness 28–9; popular
  culture 51; United States of
  America 55; working class 28
cutting and pasting 89–90

Darwin, Charles 79
democracy 22–3
Denning, Michael 55
desire 87–8
diasporic communities 61
difference 115
DiMaggio, Paul 32–3, 39–40, 45
dislocation 115–16
Docker, John 69

Dorson, Richard M. 6, 7
dress style 103–4
Du Gay, Paul 60
Duncan, Andrew 67
Dylan, Bob 63

economic determinism xi, 57–8
education: civilization 20; culture
  27; folk song 12–13; Leavisites
  24; opera 74; social class 19–20,
  94
electronic media 107
Eliot, T. S. 26, 71
elite: Boston 33–4; culture 17–18,
  21–2, 30, 41; ideology 56; opera
  125n4; Shakespeare 36; United
  States of America 37–8
elitism 59, 64
encoding/decoding 60
Engel, Carl 2
English language 49
English Premier League football
  108–9
entertainment/art 74, 76–7
entrepreneurship 32–3, 50
equality of opportunity 26–7
ethnography 61–2
eugenics 123n1
Europe 26, 36–7
evaluation 104–5, 106
Evans, David T. 76, 127n1
Evans, Dylan 128n4
evolution, theory of 79
exchange value 57
eyewitness testimony 84

family history research 129n5
fan culture 90–1
fashion 70, 103–4
Featherstone, Mike 69
Ferguson, Marjorie 54

film: audience 28, 98–9; box-office successes 96; bricolage 70–1, 72; kick-boxing 96; Kung Fu 114; narrative action 72; nostalgia 66–7, 71; readings 98–9; reproduction 27; viewing figures 96–7; Westerns 98

Fiske, John 97–8

Floyd, Nigel 67

folk culture xi, 1; authenticity 51, 116–17; fantasy 13–14, 23–4; Germany 2–3; intellectuals 6, 14–15; Jameson 68; mass culture 118–19; nationalism 2, 4; peasantry 5–6, 10; popular culture 14; social class 1–2, 5–6

folk lore 1, 121–2n2

Folk Lore Society 7, 122n2

folk music 122n4

folk song 121–2n2; civilization 12–13; education 12–13; Herder 4–5; intellectuals 1–2; nationalism 13, 14; nature 2–3; social class 11

Folk Song Society 12, 122n5

folk tales 2, 14

food, globalization 108

football 108–9

foreignness 113–14, 119

framing 33

Frankfurt School 68, 124n3

Freud, Sigmund 79, 127n2

Frith, Simon 128n1

fundamentalism 115

Gammon, Vic 8

Garnham, Nicholas 53

German folk culture 2–3

Gillespie, Marie 61

Gilman, Benjamin Ives 125n5

global culture 109–10, 117

global/local 111, 116, 119–20, 129n3

globalization: Americanization 109–12, 113–14, 129n2; food 108; homogenization 113; hybridization 108, 113, 117; local 107–8; mobility 108–9; nationalism 107; roots 129n5; sameness/difference 114–15

glocalization 112, 120

Gobineau, Joseph Arthur 18, 122n1

Golding, Peter 53, 54

Gomme, George Laurence 7

Gone With the Wind 96

Goodwin, Andrew 71

Gosse, Edmund 21

Gramsci, Antonio: cultural studies xi, 58; culture 61; economic crises 54; hegemony 48, 51, 125n2

Greenberg, Clement 41–2, 95–6, 123–4n2

Gresham's Law of culture 30

Grimm, Jacob and Wilhelm 3

Grossberg, Lawrence 68–9

Guiness World Records 96

habitus 44

Halbwachs, Maurice: collective memory 81, 82, 85; identity 86; memory as reconstruction 84, 128n5

Hall, Stuart: articulation 72, 126n3; economics 57; encoding/decoding 60; identity 79–80, 81; meaning 52; political economy 58; *The Popular Arts* 102; popular culture 51, 54; teenage culture 61, 104

Hammerstein, Oscar 38

Harker, Dave 5

Harrison, George 129n1

Hart, Walter Morris 5

Harvey, David 107

Hebdige, Dick 65

hegemony: consensus 49; cultural
  studies 53; culture 111; Gramsci
  48, 51, 125n2; leadership 50;
  popular culture 51; truth xi
Henderson, W. J. 38–9
Herder, Johann Gottfried 2–3, 4–5,
  121n1
heritage sites 85
high culture: Boston 32–4; capitalism
  64; cultural studies 93–4; low
  culture 63; mass culture 31, 41,
  69; mass media 95; opera 37–8,
  39–40, 45–6, 76, 77; popular
  culture 32, 45, 63–4, 99–100,
  106; Shakespeare 45–6; social class
  32–4; United States of America 40
history 98–9
Hoggart, Richard 59, 60
homogenization 113
Hong Kong film industry 114
Horkheimer, Max 27–8, 29, 30, 100
Howitt, Mary 121–2n2
Huyssen, Andreas 41, 42, 64, 69
hybridization: culture 108, 115, 117,
  118–19; globalization 108, 113,
  117
hyperconsciousness 72
hyperdemocracy 25

identity: consumption 78–9, 89;
  cultural consumption 78–9; culture
  81–2, 88; Hall 79–80, 81; memory
  83, 86; mirror stage 87, 90;
  multiple 80; negotiations 80–1;
  performative 91; pop music 103;
  postmodernism 79–81; subject
  position 81
ideology x, 50, 56, 101, 110–11
imaginary the 87–8, 90
imitation 66
imports, cultural 115–16

incorporation 49, 61
industrialization 3–4, 6, 10, 14, 16
infants 86–7
information, post-event 84
intellectuals 50; folk culture 6, 14–15;
  popular culture 1, 14–15, 69,
  121n1
interpellation 80–1
intertextuality 72

Jameson, Fredric: cultural pessimism
  68; folk culture 68; high/mass
  culture 69; nostalgia film 66–7, 71;
  pastiche 65–6; popular culture 68;
  postmodernism 65, 68; taste 69
Janowitz, Anne 124n1
Jenkins, Henry 90–1
Johnson, Richard 60
Johnson, Samuel 8
Jones, Greta 122–3n1

Katz, Elihu 111
Kern, Roger M. 47
kick-boxing films 96
kitsch 29, 123–4n2
Kolodin, Irving 124n4
Kristeva, Julia 90
Kung Fu films 114

Lacan, Jacques 65, 86–7, 128n4
Landsberg, Alison 85
Lang, Andrew 7
language 79, 87
language culture 49
leadership 48–9, 50
Leavis, F. R. 21, 22, 23–4, 69
Leavis, Q. D. 21–3, 23
Leavisites 21, 24
legitimacy 94, 105
Levine, Lawrence W. 34–5, 36, 37,
  38, 40

Liebes, Tamar 111
Lind, Jenny 37
Lipscomb, A. A. 36
literature 21–2
local 107–8, 116–17; *see also* global/
    local
Loftus, Elisabeth F. 82–3, 84
London Eugenics Education Society
    123n1
love 88
Lovell, Terry 57
low culture/high culture 63
Lyotard, Jean-François 64

McConachie, Bruce A. 37–8
Macdonald, Dwight 29–30
McDonalds 129n3
McLuhan, Marshall 109
McRobbie, Angela 56
Marcuse, Herbert 28
market economy 42, 54, 110–11
Marshall, Alfred 122–3n1
Martin-Barbero, Jesus 14, 126n4
Marx, Karl x, 57, 60, 79, 126n4, 128n3
mass culture: Arnold 16–17;
    commodification 68–9;
    consumption 100; corruption
    22; dominant class 46–7; Europe
    26; folk culture 118–19; high
    culture 31, 41, 69; ideology 101;
    modernism 64; nature 10; popular
    culture 20, 30–1; social class 1–2,
    46–7
mass media 85, 95
masses, deception of 28
Massey, Doreen 115–16
materiality of text 98–9
meanings x–xi, 52, 58, 84, 98
media 61, 72–3, 74, 85, 95, 107
memory: collective 81–2, 85;
    eyewitness testimony 84; false

82–3; Freud 127n2; Halbwachs 81,
    82, 84, 85, 128n5; identity 83, 86;
    individual 81–2; national 84–5;
    popular culture 85; prosthetic 85;
    reconstruction 84, 128n5; script
    86; sites of 85; trauma 82–3, 85–6
memory fetishism 127–8n3
memory industry 85–6
Metropolitan Opera (New York)
    38–9, 124n4
Michaelis-Jena, Ruth 3
middle class 11, 20, 34
mirror stage 87, 90
misrecognition 87
mobility, globalization 108–9
modernism: art 42; culture 32, 41;
    elitism 64; mass culture 64;
    self-image 42
Morley, David 58, 114, 129n2
Motherwell, William 5
Muir, Edwin 124n3
multinationals: *see* transnational
    corporations
Murdock, Graham 53, 54
Museum of Fine Arts, Boston 33,
    125n5
museums 33, 85, 125n5
music hall 11
music industry 75
Myers, Mike 67, 73

nationalism: folk culture 2, 4; folk
    song 13, 14; globalization 107;
    popular culture 1; re-emergence
    115
nature 2–3, 9–10, 10, 127[6]n1
Nava, Mica 61
need/desire 88
New York Evening Post 124n4
New York Times 38
news on television 107–8

Nickelodeon 72–3
nomadism 117
Nora, Pierre 85
Northern Star 124n1
nostalgia films 66–7, 71

objects/subjects 87, 88
Open University 60
opera: advertising use 74; CD
    collections 75; civilization 39;
    consumption 77; elite 125n4; high
    culture 37–8, 39–40, 45–6, 76,
    77; music industry 75; popular
    culture 74; postmodernism 76–7;
    social class 36–40, 75–6; United
    States of America 37, 38–9
Opera 75, 127[5]n1
opera houses 77
opera stars 74, 75–6
Ortega y Gasset, José 24–6, 42
other 87, 90

Palmer, Martyn 67
parody 34, 73
Parry, Sir Hubert 11
passivity of consumption 52–3, 111
pastiche 65–6, 70, 71
pastoralism 14
patriotism 13
Pavarotti, Luciano 75–6
peasantry 5–8, 10, 14–15, 122n3
Peggy Sue Got Married 66
Percy, Thomas 2
performance 91
Peterson, Richard 46, 47
Piaget, Jean 82
Pieterse, Jan Nederveen 113, 117–19
Platoon 86
pluralism 108
political economy 53–4, 55–6, 58,
    61–2

politics 62, 124n3, 126n4
Pop Art movement 63
pop music 63, 71, 89–90, 103
popular art 101, 102–3
The Popular Arts (Hall & Whannel)
    102–3
popular culture xi, 32, 121n1;
    aesthetics 92, 105; capitalism 51;
    consumption 97–8; convergence/
    difference 98; culture industry 51;
    evaluation 104–5, 106; folk culture
    14; hegemony 51; high culture
    32, 45, 63–4, 99–100, 106;
    intellectuals 1, 14–15, 69, 121n1;
    Jameson 68; market place 54;
    mass culture 20, 30–1; memory
    85; nationalism 1; opera 74;
    performance 91; postmodernism
    70; power xii; production in use
    52–3; ruling class 101; Shakespeare
    35; structure/agency 51; textuality
    103; working class 59–60
postmodernism 64, 72–3; bricolage
    72; capitalism, late 65;
    commodification 68; identity
    79–81; Jameson 65, 68; new
    sensibility 63–4, 69; opera 76–7;
    popular culture 70; schizophrenic
    culture 65; triviality 68
power x; agency 93; culture xi, 48,
    54, 62, 92, 94, 101, 106; global/
    local 111; popular culture xii;
    social class 14–15
power geometry 115–16
primitivism 6–9
production: art 100; consumption 57,
    60, 79, 83, 89; cultural studies 60;
    reproduction 43
production in use 52–3
profit, capitalism 56–7
Punjabi Londoners 61

race 18, 25–6, 123n1
radio 28
Raynor, Henry 37
RCA Victor 39
re-activation 71
readings of film 98–9
realism: affective 90; emotional 103; false 67
reconstruction 83
recycling 70, 71–2
religious fundamentalism 115
remembering 83, 84; *see also* memory
Renan, Ernest 18
representation x, 80–1, 83
reproduction 27, 43
resistance 49, 61, 69
Ritzer, George 129n4
Robertson, Roland 112
rock music 101
romantic love 88
Romanticism 1, 9–10
roots 129n5
Rumble Fish 66

sacralization 33, 125n5
Said, Edward 117
sameness 115
sampling, pop music 71
Saussure, Ferdinand de 79
savages 6–8
Schiller, Herbert 109
script/memory 86
self: becoming 80; consumption 89; decentred 79; desire 87–8; identity 79–81; modernism 42; other 87
sensibility, new 63–4, 69
Shakespeare, William: elite 36; *Hamlet* 34; high culture 45–6; *Othello* 34–5; parodies 34; popular culture 35; *Richard III* 34; social class 35–6, 124n1; United States of America 34
Shakespeareanism 36
Sharp, Cecil James 2, 5–6, 8–9, 12–13
Shusterman, Richard 99, 101, 102
Simkus, Albert 46
The Simpsons 72
Smith, Barbara Herrnstein 92–3
social authority 30
social class: cultural consumption 44, 47; culture 10–11, 17–18, 26, 43, 44–7; dominant 46–7, 94, 101; education 19–20, 94; folk culture 1–2, 5–6; folk song 11; high culture 32–4; leadership 48–9; mass culture 1–2, 46–7; opera 36–40, 75–6; popular culture 101; power relations 14–15; Shakespeare 35–6, 124n1; taste 21–2, 45–7; tradition 93; Williams xi–xii; *see also* middle class; working class
social construction xi, 52
social control 31
social status 97
Sontag, Susan 63
Spanish women 114
Springfield, Dusty 89–90, 91
Star Wars trilogy 66
state apparatus 50
Storey, John xi, 50, 51, 53, 63, 72, 101, 104
Street, John 128n1
structure/agency 51, 55, 60, 72–3
Sturken, Marita 86
subject/object 81, 87
superficiality 66
surplus value 57
symbolic the 87–8

Tarantino, Quentin 71
taste: classification 43–4; consumption 97; Jameson 69; literature 21–2; natural 94; social class 21–2, 45–7; social status 97
teenage culture 61, 103–4
television news 107–8
text xi, 90–1, 98–9, 105, 126n3
textuality 103
Thompson, Denys 21, 22, 23–4
Thoms, W. J. 121–2n2
time–space compression 107, 115
Titanic 96
Toledo, Archbishop of 114
Tomlinson, John 110, 114, 119, 120
Towle, George Makepeace 37
tradition 93
transnational corporations 107, 109, 110
trauma 82–3, 85–6
truth x, xi
Turner, Bryan 69
Twin Peaks 72
Tylor, Sir Edward Burnet 6–7

unconsciousness 79
United States of America: commodities 112; culture industry 55; elite 37–8; high culture 40; interpretations of history 98–9; opera 37, 38–9; Shakespeare 34; transnational corporations 110; *see also* Americanization

urbanization 3–4, 6, 10, 14, 16
use value 57

valorization of culture 100–1
values/aesthetics 105
Vaughan Williams, Ralph 7–8, 122n4
Vickers, John 75
Vietnam War 86
Volosinov, Valentin 83, 126n3

Western films 98
Whannel, Paddy 61, 102
Wheeler, A. C. 36
White, Richard Grant 36
"Whole Again" (Atomic Kitten) 88
Williams, Raymond x, xi–xii, 59–60, 93
Willis, Paul 56
Wilson, Elizabeth 70
Wolff, Janet 40
Wordsworth, William 9–10
workers 10–11, 57
working class: Arnold 23; culture 10–11, 14, 20; culture industry 28; popular culture 59–60; urban-industrial 10, 14, 16
world music 113

Young, Robert J. C. 18

Zelochow, Bernard 36, 37